THE ULTIMATE
RECIPES ACROSS AMERICA
COOKBOOK

The paper in this printing meets the requirements of the ANSI Standard Z39.48-1992.

Photos on page vi, 58, 90, and 184 used with permission from Kelly Rusin. Photos on page vi and 120 used with permission from Jodi Flayman.
USA Word Map:
Copyright: <a href='https://www.123rf.com/profile_tupungato'>tupungato / 123RF Stock Photo</a>
Las Vegas sign:
Copyright: <a href='https://www.123rf.com/profile_somchaij'>somchaij / 123RF Stock Photo</a>
Route 66:
Copyright: <a href='https://www.123rf.com/profile_duha127'>duha127 / 123RF Stock Photo</a>
Texas sign:
Copyright: <a href='https://www.123rf.com/profile_andreykr'>andreykr / 123RF Stock Photo</a>
Yellowstone National Park sign:
Copyright: <a href='https://www.123rf.com/profile_pabrady63'>pabrady63 / 123RF Stock Photo</a>
Barn Photo:
Copyright: <a href='https://www.123rf.com/profile_dcwcreations'>dcwcreations / 123RF Stock Photo</a>
Nashville Tennessee Road Sign image credit: snoopydog1955 / Pond5

While every care has been taken in compiling the recipes for this book, the publisher, Cogin, Inc., or any other person who has been involved in working on this publication assumes no responsibility or liability for any errors or omissions, inadvertent or not, that may be found in the recipes or text, nor for any problems or damages that may arise as a result of preparing these recipes.

If food allergies or dietary restrictions are a concern, it is recommended that you carefully read ingredient product labels as well as consult a nutritionist or your physician to determine if a particular recipe meets your dietary needs.

We encourage you to use caution when working with all kitchen equipment and to always follow food safety guidelines.

To purchase this book for business or promotional use or to purchase more than 50 copies at a discount, or for custom editions, please contact Cogin, Inc. at the address below or info@mrfood.com.

Inquiries should be addressed to:
Cogin, Inc.
1770 NW 64 Street, Suite 500
Fort Lauderdale, FL 33309

ISBN: 978-0-9981635-1-2
Printed in the United States of America
First Edition
www.MrFood.com

Introduction

What is your state famous for? Is it Southern fried chicken with a crunch so loud that it can be heard across the room, Key lime pie that makes you feel like you're sitting on a dock in Key West, or Texas beef brisket that's coated in the perfect rub? When it comes to cooking, every state and region across the country is known for having recipes that are unique to them. That's why the Mr. Food Test Kitchen scoured the country in search of the most authentic foods from coast to coast. Once we found the best of the best, we recreated those tastes by developing an easy-as-can-be recipe, and then we tasted and tweaked each one to make sure they'll work flawlessly in your kitchen.

Our recipes make it easy for you to take a culinary road trip across the country without ever having to leave your kitchen. You'll be able to enjoy a sunny California favorite from your cozy Carolina kitchen. On top of that, we've included the stories behind the recipes along with fun anecdotes that'll make you smile. So, not only will you get to whip up something delicious, but you'll have plenty to talk about while at the dinner table.

No matter where you grew up or where you're currently living, you're going to love these quick and easy, favorite American recipes made from off-the-shelf ingredients and featuring simple, step-by-step instructions. And to tempt your taste buds even more, we've included a full-page photo for each one of our 130+ recipes!

So, join the Mr. Food Test Kitchen Team as we share America's best homegrown recipes. Whether you start with Alaska or Wyoming makes no difference, since every recipe is sure to have you saying...

"OOH IT'S SO GOOD!!®"

Acknowledgements

America is full of tasty treasures, and we're so thankful for the talented team that helped bring all of them together.

Patty Rosenthal
Test Kitchen Director

Kelly Rusin
Photographer & Stylist

Howard Rosenthal
Chief Food Officer

Jodi Flayman
Director of Publishing

Merly Mesa
Editor

Victoria Krog
Photo Assistant

Amy Magro
Dir. of Business Affairs

Jaime Gross
Business Assistant

Carol Ginsburg
Editor

Steve Ginsburg
Chief Executive Officer

Dave DiCarlo
Test Kitchen Assistant

Roxana DeLima
Comptroller

Hal Silverman
Pre-Press Production
Hal Silverman Studio

Lorraine Dan
Book Design
Grand Design

Table of Contents

As always, we remember our founder, Art Ginsburg, who believed that everyone would cook if only we could make it "quick & easy." We thank you for allowing us to carry on this tradition.

Welcome to the Mr. Food Test Kitchen Family!

Whether you've been a fan of the Mr. Food Test Kitchen for years or were just recently introduced to us, we want to welcome you into our kitchen...and our family. Even though we've grown in many ways over the years, the one thing that hasn't changed is our philosophy for quick & easy cooking.

Over 40 years ago we began by sharing our recipes with you through the television screen. Today, not only is the Mr. Food Test Kitchen TV segment syndicated all over the country, but we've also proudly published over 60 best-selling cookbooks. That's not to mention the hugely popular MrFood.com and EverydayDiabeticRecipes.com. And for those of you who love to get social, we do too! You can find us online on Facebook, Twitter, Pinterest, and Instagram— boy, do we love connecting with you!

If you've got a passion for cooking (like we do!), then you know that the only thing better than curling up with a cookbook and drooling over the pictures is actually getting to taste the finished recipes. That's why we give you simple step-by-step instructions that make it feel like we're in your kitchen guiding you along the way. Your taste buds will be celebrating in no time!

Now that you're a part of the family, we hope you'll come visit us whenever we're in your neighborhood, whether it's at the local fair or some fancy-dancy event. We love getting to meet you personally, so be sure to introduce yourself! And don't forget to bring a camera and this book, because we'll definitely want to take some photos and leave you with a special signed message.

You can bet there's always room at our table for you, because there's nothing better than sharing in all of the... "OOH IT'S SO GOOD!!®"

Kelly   Howard   Patty

A Bit About This Book

When we're traveling around the country, one of our favorite things to do is to eat where the locals eat, so that we can experience the true tastes of the area. We also thank all of our friends at TV stations around the country for introducing us to the local fare whenever we come to visit. We cherish those meals and the stories behind each one of them. After discovering so many great foods during our travels (many of which we'd never even heard about!), we knew we needed to share them with you. Although we've made every effort to keep these as authentic as possible, we did take a few shortcuts, to keep the recipes quick & easy so that you can make them using off-the-shelf ingredients.

We also realize that there are many interpretations on how these dishes should be prepared. So, if you see your local favorite and it's not exactly what you grew up with or how you remember it...no problem! Feel free to tweak it!

Other titles you may enjoy from the
Mr. Food Test Kitchen:

Christmas Made Easy

Quick & Easy Comfort Cookbook

Sinful Sweets & Tasty Treats

Just One More Bite!

Hello Taste, Goodbye Guilt! (Diabetic Friendly)

Guilt-Free Weeknight Favorites (Diabetic Friendly)

Cook it Slow, Cook it Fast

Wheel of Fortune Collectible Cookbook

The Ultimate Cooking for Two Cookbook

The Ultimate Cake Mix & More Cookbook

The Ultimate 30 Minutes or Less Cookbook

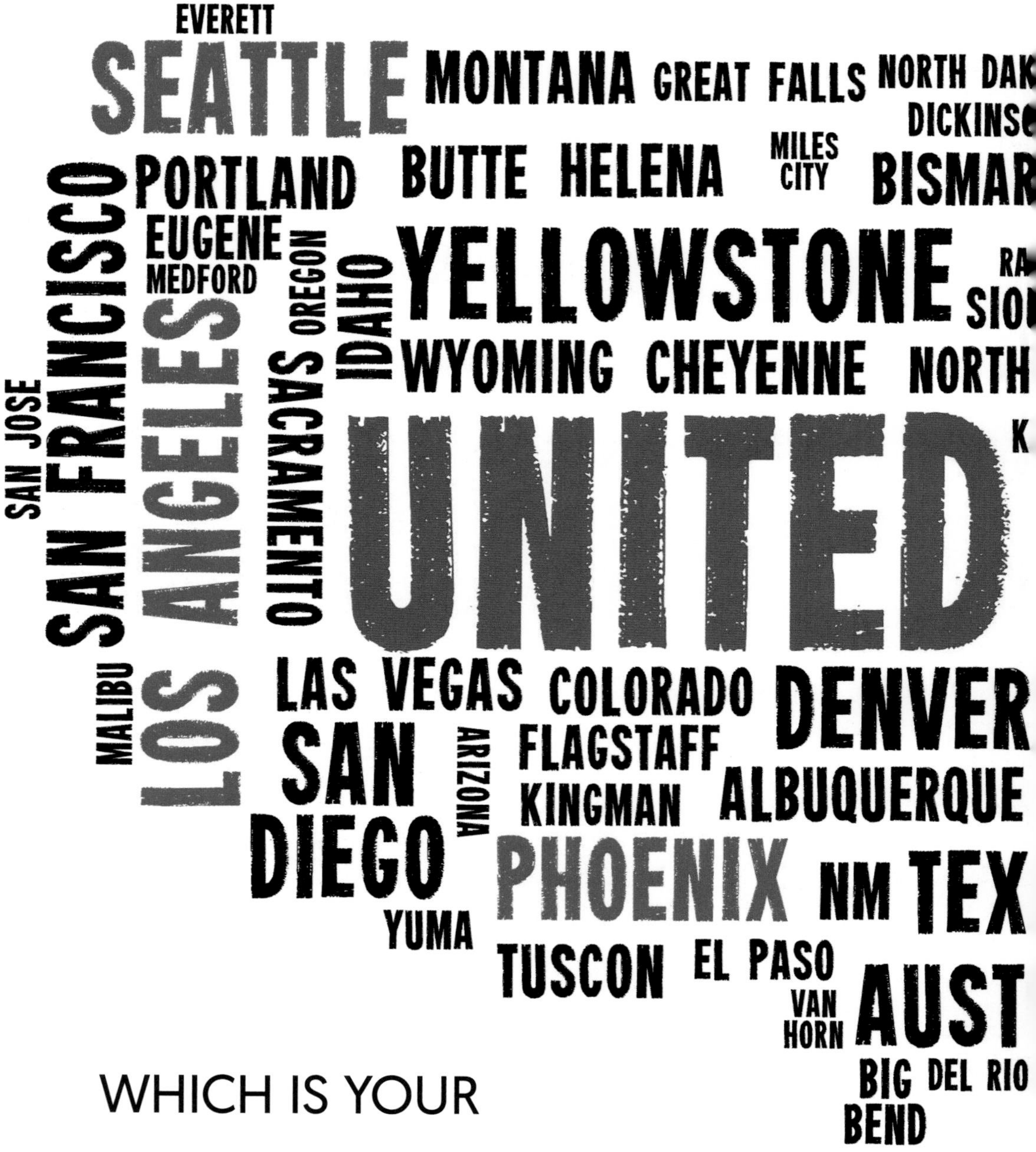

EVERETT
SEATTLE MONTANA GREAT FALLS NORTH DAK
DICKINSO
PORTLAND BUTTE HELENA MILES CITY BISMAR
EUGENE
MEDFORD OREGON IDAHO YELLOWSTONE RA
SIO
SAN JOSE SAN FRANCISCO WYOMING CHEYENNE NORTH
SACRAMENTO K
ANGELES UNITED
MALIBU LOS LAS VEGAS COLORADO DENVER
SAN ARIZONA FLAGSTAFF
DIEGO KINGMAN ALBUQUERQUE
YUMA PHOENIX NM TEX
TUSCON EL PASO AUST
VAN HORN
BIG DEL RIO
BEND

WHICH IS YOUR

FAVORITE

FOOD CITY?

MINNESOTA
BEMIDJI
BRAINERD ST.PAUL GREEN BAY
DULUTH MARQUETTE
GRAND RAPIDS
MINNEAPOLIS SAGINAW MI
DETROIT
LANSING
ALBANY
NEW YORK
NIAGARA BUFFALO
BOSTON
ORONO ACADIA NP
MAINE
BANGOR

CHICAGO
INDIANA WASHINGTON DC
PHILADELPHIA

STATES
RICHMOND
CHARLESTON
CHARLOTTE RALEIGH

SPRINGFIELD ARKANSAS ATLANTA
COLUMBIA
NC
SC
FAYETTEVILLE CONWAY
MEMPHIS TN
FORT WORTH LITTLE ROCK
MONTGOMERY
SHREVEPORT
DALLAS JACKSON TALLAHASSEE SAVANNAH
ANTONIO HOUSTON BATON ROUGE
GALVESTON
TAMPA
MIAMI

After ordering cinnamon buns in Texas, we understand why they say "everything's bigger in Texas." Find out for yourself on page 2!

Howard was all smiles as he chowed down on a potato donut in Maine. Check out page 28 for the recipe and soon you'll be all smiles!

We had a blast picking apples at the apple orchard. We also had our fair share of apple fritters and fresh pressed cider. We were stuffed!

Some of our travels led us to really "egg-citing" places, like an egg farm where we got to eat a real farm-to-table breakfast!

Things got a little spicy in New York's Chelsea Market (home to the Food Network). We were in heaven.

Eye-Opening Breakfasts

Texas-Style Cinnamon Buns

The Texas State Fair is the country's biggest fair, so you can bet that they've got a huge assortment of fair foods for visitors to munch on. While anything deep fried gets lots of "oohs" and "ahhs," there's one tried-and-true favorite that never gets passed by: the cinnamon buns. Like everything in Texas, these cinnamon buns are anything but small. Soft, nutty, and topped with a sweet and creamy icing, these buns are great for either breakfast or dessert.

Makes 6

Ingredients

1 cup light brown sugar

1 tablespoon ground cinnamon

¾ cup chopped walnuts

1 pound frozen bread dough, thawed

1 stick butter, softened

ICING
½ cup confectioners' sugar

3 tablespoons heavy cream

Preparation

1 Coat a 7- x 11-inch baking dish with cooking spray.

2 In a small bowl, combine brown sugar, cinnamon, and walnuts; set aside.

3 On a lightly floured surface, roll dough into a 10- x 15-inch rectangle. Spread dough with butter and sprinkle evenly with brown sugar mixture. Roll up dough tightly in jelly-roll fashion. Cut into 6 rolls and place cut-side up in baking dish. Cover with plastic wrap and let rise at room temperature 60 to 90 minutes or until doubled in size.

4 Preheat oven to 350 degrees F. Remove plastic wrap and bake rolls 20 to 25 minutes or until golden. Let cool slightly.

5 To make icing, in a small bowl, whisk confectioners' sugar and heavy cream until smooth. Spread over cinnamon buns and serve warm.

Midwest Diner Hoppel Poppel

This is the ultimate, one skillet, kitchen sink breakfast and no, we don't have a clue as to what "hoppel poppel" actually means. What we do know is that this hearty breakfast can be found on diner menus all across the Midwest. It's based off of a German-style breakfast that's made using potatoes, eggs, and meat, with the potatoes and meat usually being the leftovers from the night before. This one is hearty, so make sure your family brings their appetite!

Serves 6

Ingredients

½ stick butter

1-½ pounds boiled potatoes, cut into 1-inch chunks

¾ cup chopped onion

½ teaspoon salt

¼ teaspoon black pepper

½ pound smoked kielbasa, sliced into ¼-inch pieces

½ pound leftover cooked meat, cut into ½-inch pieces (see note)

6 eggs

2 tablespoons room temperature water

Preparation

1 In a large skillet over medium-high heat, melt butter. Add potatoes and onion, season with salt and pepper, and sauté 10 minutes or until golden, stirring occasionally. Stir in kielbasa and cooked meat and heat 5 minutes, stirring occasionally.

2 In a medium bowl, whisk eggs and water; pour over the potato and meat mixture. Carefully stir until eggs are set. Serve immediately.

So Many Options: *For the meat, feel free to use cooked pork, roast beef, chicken, or whatever else you have in the fridge. Each time you make it, it might be a little different, but it'll always be tasty!*

Blueberry Buttermilk Pancakes

Wild blueberries are native to Maine, where you'll find acres and acres of them growing. In fact, the area is sometimes called the "Land of Wild Blueberries." The wild blueberry is a little smaller than the more common highbush blueberry, but that doesn't make it any less flavorful. These pea-sized berries pack an intense punch of sweet and tangy flavor that doesn't go unnoticed. That may be why they make such a tasty addition to these fluffy buttermilk pancakes!

Makes 12

Ingredients

2 cups all-purpose flour

2 tablespoons sugar

2 teaspoons baking powder

1 teaspoon baking soda

1 teaspoon salt

2 eggs

2 cups buttermilk

1 teaspoon vanilla extract

2 tablespoons butter, melted, plus extra for cooking

1 cup fresh blueberries

Preparation

1 In a large bowl, combine flour, sugar, baking powder, baking soda, and salt; mix well.

2 In a medium bowl, whisk eggs, buttermilk, vanilla, and 2 tablespoons melted butter; stir into dry ingredients just until combined. Do not overmix. Stir in blueberries.

3 On a griddle or in a skillet over medium heat, melt 1 tablespoon butter. Pour $1/3$ cup batter onto griddle pan and cook 2 to 3 minutes or until bubbles begin to form. Turn and cook 1 to 2 additional minutes or until golden brown. Repeat with remaining batter, adding more butter as needed. Serve immediately.

Test Kitchen Tip: *You can use any tasty variety of blueberries to make these, however, if you want something special, make sure you pick up some wild blueberries from Maine.*

The Great Big Denver Omelet

If you head over to California Street in Downtown Denver, you'll find a plaque embedded in the sidewalk with the basic recipe for The Denver Omelet. According to the plaque, "The Denver omelet was developed to mask the stale flavor of eggs shipped by wagon freight." What the plaque doesn't mention is that this morning favorite actually started out as a sandwich; the same omelet, just stuffed between two slices of toast. Today, it's typically served with the toast on the side.

Serves 2

Ingredients

3 tablespoons butter, divided

¼ cup diced green bell pepper

2 tablespoons diced onion

½ cup chopped cooked ham

4 eggs

2 tablespoons room temperature water (see Tip)

¼ teaspoon salt

¼ teaspoon black pepper

½ cup shredded cheddar cheese

Preparation

1 In a medium skillet over medium heat, melt 2 tablespoons butter. Add bell pepper, onion, and ham and sauté 4 to 5 minutes or until vegetables are tender. Remove vegetable mixture from skillet and set aside.

2 Melt remaining 1 tablespoon butter in skillet. In a bowl, beat eggs with water, salt, and pepper. Add to skillet and, with a rubber spatula, gently stir, pushing the cooked portion of the eggs to the center of the skillet, letting uncooked egg run to the edge of skillet.

3 When the eggs firm up and are no longer runny, sprinkle half the omelet with cheese and top with vegetable mixture. Cook until cheese is melted. To serve, slide omelet onto a platter, folding the half without the filling over the half with it. Cut in half and serve.

Test Kitchen Tip: *When making omelets or scrambling eggs, we suggest beating the eggs with warm or room temperature water, rather than milk or cold water. By doing so, we end up with a fluffier omelet.*

Breakfast Biscuits with Sausage Gravy

Walk into any Southern-style restaurant for breakfast and you're sure to see biscuits and gravy on the menu. It's a popular dish that started who knows when and has become a hearty morning favorite. Depending on where you go you might get served milk gravy, sawmill gravy, or sausage gravy. While they're all good, we went with a heartier sausage gravy for this one. Serve it with a heapin' helping of scrambled eggs for even more fill-ya-up goodness!

Serves 6

Ingredients

2-¼ cups pancake and biscuit mix

⅔ cup plus 1-½ cups milk, divided

2 tablespoons melted butter

1 (16-ounce) tube hot pork sausage (see Tip)

3 tablespoons all-purpose flour

1 tablespoon Worcestershire sauce

¼ teaspoon salt

¼ teaspoon black pepper

Preparation

1 Preheat oven to 450 degrees F.

2 In a large bowl, combine biscuit mix, ⅔ cup milk, and the butter; stir until thoroughly blended. Drop 6 equal spoonfuls of dough onto a baking sheet. Bake 8 to 10 minutes or until golden.

3 Meanwhile, in a large skillet over medium-high heat, cook sausage 6 to 8 minutes or until no pink remains, stirring to crumble sausage. Add flour; mix well. Add Worcestershire sauce and the remaining 1-½ cups milk, the salt, and pepper; mix well. Cook 2 to 4 minutes or until gravy thickens, stirring constantly. Serve over biscuits.

Test Kitchen Tip: *To keep this as authentic as possible, make sure to use the pork sausage that comes in a tube, not the hot Italian pork sausage from the meat case.*

Santa Fe Breakfast Burritos

In New Mexico, the breakfast burrito is the breakfast of choice, especially if you're in Santa Fe, where it was allegedly born. While there are no specific rules about what goes in these burritos, you'll generally find some combination of eggs, meat, breakfast-style potatoes, and green chiles (you can't forget these!). Green chiles are grown in New Mexico and are a staple in many of the state's most popular foods. These will definitely add a kick to your morning!

Serves 4

Ingredients

3 tablespoons vegetable oil

2-½ cups refrigerated shredded potatoes

¼ cup chopped onion

¼ teaspoon salt

¼ teaspoon black pepper

6 eggs

2 tablespoons butter

4 (10-inch) spinach-flavored flour tortillas, warmed

1 (4-ounce) can green chiles, drained

8 slices crispy cooked bacon

2 cups shredded Colby-Jack cheese

Sriracha sauce for drizzling (optional)

Preparation

1 In a medium skillet over medium-high heat, heat oil until hot; add potatoes, onion, salt, and pepper. Cook 8 to 10 minutes or until crispy brown; set aside.

2 In a medium bowl, beat eggs. In a large skillet over medium heat, melt butter. Add eggs and scramble 3 to 5 minutes or until eggs are set.

3 In the center of each tortilla, evenly top with potatoes, eggs, green chiles, bacon, and cheese. Fold bottom half of tortilla over filling, then fold in sides and roll up. Cut in half and drizzle with sriracha sauce, if desired. Serve immediately.

Test Kitchen Tip: *The best way to warm the tortillas is to wrap them in foil and pop them in a 300 degree oven for about 5 minutes. That will make them nice and pliable, and easy to roll.*

Cornmeal Scrapple

The "scrap" in "scrapple" gives you a good clue about how this Pennsylvania breakfast came to be. Originally, this dish was created as a way to use up every last bit of a pig. Cornmeal was also added to help thicken up the cooked mixture before it was shaped, sliced, and fried (or eaten as-is). The good news is, nowadays, you don't have to wait for scraps to enjoy a slice of flavorful fried scrapple.

Makes 8 slices

Ingredients

½ pound ground pork breakfast sausage

1-¾ cups chicken broth or water

1-¾ cups milk

1 cup cornmeal

½ teaspoon poultry seasoning

½ teaspoon salt

¼ teaspoon black pepper

3 tablespoons butter

Preparation

1 Coat an 8- x 4-inch loaf pan with cooking spray.

2 In a large skillet over medium-high heat, cook sausage 5 to 7 minutes or until browned, stirring occasionally; drain off fat. Add broth and milk; bring to a boil. Stir in cornmeal, poultry seasoning, salt, and pepper, and cook until thickened. Reduce heat to low, cover, and cook 10 minutes, stirring occasionally.

3 Pour into loaf pan, cool slightly, and refrigerate at least 2 hours. Invert onto a board, and cut into 1-inch-thick slices.

4 In a large skillet over medium heat, melt butter; cook slices 8 to 10 minutes or until golden brown on both sides, turning halfway through cooking.

Serving Suggestion: Although many have personal preferences, there are many ways to top this hog-heavenly delight. You can drizzle on honey or syrup, squirt it with ketchup or mustard, or slather it with apple butter.

Apple Orchard Maple French Toast

There are over 100 varieties of apples easily available in markets around the country. That's because the U.S. is the second largest producer of apples in the world, with Washington, New York, and Michigan being the top three growing states. It's not surprising that Americans have come up with thousands of different ways to enjoy apples at every mealtime, including breakfast. You'll be sure to rouse everyone from their beds with the smell of this apple-y syrup cooking on the stove.

Serves 4

Ingredients

1 loaf homestyle bread, not sliced

7 tablespoons butter, divided

2 apples, peeled, cored, and diced

1 cup maple syrup

1 teaspoon vanilla extract

1-½ teaspoons ground cinnamon, divided

8 eggs

¼ cup milk

¼ teaspoon salt

Preparation

1 Preheat oven to 375 degrees F. Cut bread into 8 (1-inch-thick) slices.

2 In a medium saucepan over medium heat, melt 4 tablespoons butter. Add apples and cook 5 minutes, stirring occasionally. Stir in syrup, vanilla, and ½ teaspoon cinnamon; reduce heat to low and simmer 8 to 10 minutes or until apples are tender. Set aside and keep warm.

3 Meanwhile, in a medium bowl, whisk eggs, milk, remaining 1 teaspoon cinnamon, and the salt.

4 On a griddle or griddle pan over medium heat, melt remaining 3 tablespoons butter. Dip each slice of bread into the egg mixture, making sure the bread is completely coated. Cook in batches 2 to 4 minutes or until golden on both sides, turning halfway through cooking. Place French toast on baking sheet. Repeat with remaining bread.

5 Bake 8 to 10 minutes or until center is cooked through. Serve with warmed apple syrup.

Rhode Island's Johnnycakes

Johnnycakes are a type of cornmeal pancake, and they date back to a time before the arrival of European settlers. It's said that they were first created by Native Americans who had been cooking with ground corn for years. While they're eaten in several states, Rhode Islanders have a special place in their hearts and on their plates for johnnycakes. They've found a way to eat them at any time of the day!

Makes 10

Ingredients

2 cups self-rising cornmeal

¾ teaspoon salt

1 cup boiling water

¼ cup milk

3 tablespoons butter

Preparation

1 In a large bowl, combine cornmeal and salt. Gradually stir in boiling water and milk; mix until well combined.

2 Heat a griddle pan or skillet over medium heat until hot. Melt 1 tablespoon butter, then drop ¼ cup batter per pancake onto griddle pan. Cook 2 to 3 minutes per side or until golden brown. Repeat with remaining batter, adding more butter as needed. Serve immediately.

Serving Suggestion: A little syrup or butter makes these extra-delicious. Serve them alongside your favorite breakfast go-alongs (bacon!) for a hearty start to your day.

New Jersey Breakfast Sandwiches

In the late 19th century a man named John Taylor came up with a recipe for meat that was a little like bologna, salami, and Canadian bacon all in one. He called it "Taylor's Prepared Ham." Since it was found that the meat couldn't legally be called ham, the name was changed to "Taylor's Pork Roll." Nowadays, folks in north Jersey refer to it as Taylor Ham, while folks in south Jersey call it a pork roll. Both will agree that it's a breakfast favorite.

Serves 2

Ingredients

4 slices Taylor ham

2 tablespoons butter, divided

2 eggs

Salt and pepper for sprinkling

2 crusty rolls, cut in half and toasted

2 slices American cheese

Preparation

1 Place ham on a small cutting board and cut 4 [¼-inch] slits around the edges of each slice. [This will prevent it from curling when cooked.] In a large skillet over medium heat, melt 1 tablespoon butter; sauté ham 4 to 6 minutes or until browned around edges, turning once during cooking. Remove to a plate and cover to keep warm.

2 In the same skillet, melt remaining 1 tablespoon butter; crack eggs into the pan, leaving some room between them so they don't cook together. Cook 2 minutes, lightly sprinkle with salt and pepper, flip eggs over, and cook until desired doneness.

3 Place 2 slices of ham on bottom half of each roll, then top each with an egg and slice of cheese. Place top of rolls over cheese and serve immediately.

Did You Know? The cheese will melt slightly from the warmth of the egg, but if you like your cheese super melty, place the sandwich on a baking sheet and pop it in a hot oven for a couple of minutes.

Boston Brown Bread

The idea of making bread in a can dates back to the colonial years, when Native Americans showed the colonists how to steam their breads over an open fire. As stoves became commonplace, folks modernized the idea by making their breads inside tin cans and steaming them in a boiling pot of water. It's a New England tradition that you can still enjoy today.

Makes 2 loaves

Ingredients

2 (15-ounce) cans, empty and clean

½ cup rye flour

½ cup whole wheat flour

¼ cup cornmeal

2 tablespoons light brown sugar

¾ teaspoon baking powder

¼ teaspoon salt

1 cup buttermilk

½ cup molasses

1 tablespoon vegetable oil

½ cup raisins

Preparation

1 Coat inside of cans with cooking spray.

2 In a large bowl, combine rye and whole wheat flours, cornmeal, brown sugar, baking powder, and salt; mix well. Add buttermilk, molasses, and oil; whisk until smooth. Stir in raisins. Divide batter evenly between cans.

3 Place a piece of aluminum foil over the top of each can, pressing firmly around edges to secure. Place cans in a soup pot, foil wrapped-side up, and fill pot with hot water halfway up sides of cans.

4 Cover pot and bring to a boil over high heat. Reduce heat to low and simmer 35 to 40 minutes or until toothpick inserted in center of cans comes out clean. Carefully remove cans from pot to wire rack, remove foil, and let cool. Remove bread by turning cans upside down. Slice and enjoy.

Serving Suggestion: *While this is great eaten as-is, we like to slather on some butter or cream cheese, or why not try one of the homemade jam recipes on the next page.*

Strawberry Patch Refrigerator Jam

Do you ever find yourself with more strawberries than you know what to do with? That might be because more strawberries are grown in the U.S. than anywhere else in the world, and our top two growing states have opposite growing seasons, which means we can enjoy fresh strawberries year-round. The next time you find yourself overloaded with berries, don't toss them! Instead, make some homemade strawberry jam to go with your next breakfast.

Makes about 2 cups

Ingredients

1 quart fresh strawberries, washed, hulled, and quartered

3 cups sugar

¼ cup water

2 teaspoons lemon juice

Note: The amount of sugar can be decreased by ½ a cup or so if your fruit is nice and sweet.

Preparation

1 In a large saucepan over medium heat, bring all ingredients to a boil, stirring constantly. Reduce heat to low and simmer 15 to 20 minutes or until strawberries have cooked down and mixture has thickened, or until candy thermometer reaches 220 degrees F, stirring frequently. Remove from heat and allow to cool slightly.

2 Place in an airtight container or mason jar and chill at least 4 hours before serving. (Jam can be refrigerated for up to two months.)

So Many Options: Want to try this with other fresh fruit? No problem! Here are two more for you to try out:

Homemade Georgia Peach Jam: Follow the instructions above except substitute the strawberries for 10 to 12 peaches, peeled and cut into chunks, decrease the sugar to 1-½ cups, and only use 1 teaspoon of lemon juice.

Homemade Blueberry Patch Jam: Follow the instructions above except substitute the strawberries for 3 cups of fresh blueberries and add ¼ teaspoon of salt.

Mardi Gras Shortcut Beignets

Although beignets are eaten all year long in New Orleans, they're especially popular during Mardi Gras when it's traditional to eat fried foods. (The word "beignet" is actually French for "fritter.") Beignets are sometimes filled with jelly, fruit, or chocolate, but we kept ours classic with a powdered sugar topping. Serve them on their own or the way they do at the world famous Café Du Monde, with a brew of chicory and coffee.

Makes 32

Ingredients

1 (1-pound) loaf frozen bread dough, thawed

2 cups vegetable shortening

Confectioners' sugar for sprinkling

Preparation

1 Lightly flour a cutting board, and with a floured rolling pin, roll out dough to an 8- by 16-inch rectangle. Cut into 2-inch squares.

2 In a large deep skillet over medium heat, heat shortening until hot, but not smoking. Add dough squares a few at a time and cook in batches, about 30 seconds per side or until golden. Drain on a paper towel-lined baking sheet.

3 While warm, sprinkle beignets generously with confectioners' sugar. Serve warm with lots of napkins.

Did You Know? *Chicory is the root of the endive plant, and it was first added to coffee to help stretch its supply. However, in New Orleans it's as traditional as beignets. There, dark roasted coffee is blended with chicory. You can have it "black" or "au lait," which means it's mixed with hot milk.*

Cinnamon Sugar Potato Doughnuts

Doughnuts have been around since long before U.S. history began, and today they're still an American favorite. Traditionally, they're made with yeast dough, but their rise in popularity has lead to experimentation. The good news is that now, we've got potato doughnuts. Chances are, you've visited a doughnut shop before. One city where you'll find lots of delicious varieties of this "spud" nut is Portland, Maine.

Makes 1 dozen

Ingredients

3 tablespoons butter, softened

1-¼ cups sugar, divided

1 egg, at room temperature

1 teaspoon vanilla extract

1 cup lightly packed mashed potatoes (like russet)

¼ cup buttermilk

2 cups all-purpose flour, plus more for dusting

1 teaspoon baking powder

½ teaspoon baking soda

½ teaspoon salt

½ teaspoon ground nutmeg

3 cups vegetable shortening

½ teaspoon ground cinnamon

Preparation

1 In a large bowl with an electric mixer, beat butter and ¾ cup sugar until fluffy. Add egg and vanilla, and beat until well combined. Add potatoes and buttermilk and beat until smooth. Add 2 cups flour, the baking powder, baking soda, salt, and nutmeg, and beat just until evenly mixed. Do not overmix.

2 Generously dust your work surface with flour. Place dough on work surface and turn to coat with flour.

3 Gently press dough out with your hands to ½-inch thickness and cut into rounds using a 3-inch donut cutter or biscuit cutter and a 1-inch bottle cap for center hole. Gather scraps and gently press out again as needed until all dough is used.

4 In a soup pot, heat shortening over medium heat to 375 degrees F, using a thermometer. Working in small batches, cook doughnuts 2 to 3 minutes per side or until puffed and golden brown on both sides, turning once during cooking. Transfer to a paper towel-lined baking sheet.

5 In a small bowl, combine remaining ½ cup sugar with the cinnamon. When donuts are cool enough to handle, toss in sugar/cinnamon mixture. Serve warm or place in an airtight container.

No, this isn't a painting! It's a lighthouse we visited while in Maine. If it looks familiar, that's because we've heard it's the same one that they use in the Red Lobster restaurant ads.

Howard and Patty check out the Boston Harbor in between sampling everything in Faneuil Market and warming up with a bowl of clam chowda!

What happens in Vegas, stays in Vegas. Well, sort of. We did leave there with a recipe or two that we're sharing with you on page 48.

There's nothing more All-American than going to a baseball game. While we love the game, we're also big fans of the food. Check out our home run collection of hotdog recipes on page 142.

We visited a lot of farms on our travels. If you've never had the chance to visit a working farm, you really should! Our country's farmers do so much for us.

Amazing Appetizers

Chesapeake Bay Crab Cakes

During crabbing season, millions of blue crabs can be found throughout the Chesapeake Bay area. It's no wonder then that crab-anything is a Bay favorite. From crab soup to crab dip, folks have found a way to enjoy crab every which way. They especially like serving their crab in the form of cakes or patties. Served as appetizers or as a main dish, these are always welcomed with a great big smile.

Makes 20

Ingredients

- ½ cup mayonnaise
- 1 egg
- 1 tablespoon Dijon mustard
- 1 tablespoon hot sauce
- 2 cloves garlic, minced
- 1 teaspoon seafood seasoning (see Note)
- ¼ teaspoon salt
- ¼ teaspoon black pepper
- ¾ cup bread crumbs
- 1 pound lump crab meat, drained
- 4 tablespoons olive oil, divided

Preparation

1 In a large bowl, whisk together mayonnaise, egg, mustard, hot sauce, garlic, seafood seasoning, salt, and pepper. Gently stir in bread crumbs and crab until just combined. (Do not over-mix as you do not want to break up the chunks of crab.) Form into 20 crab cakes.

2 In a large skillet over medium heat, heat 2 tablespoons oil. Sauté crab cakes 3 to 4 minutes per side or until golden brown. Remove to a platter and cover with aluminum foil to keep warm. Repeat with remaining crab cakes, adding more oil as needed.

Note: As they most commonly do in the Bay area, we used Old Bay® as the seafood seasoning.

Serving Suggestion: These go great with our homemade **Mustard Dipping Sauce**. To make it, all you need to do is combine ¼ cup mayonnaise, 1 tablespoon Dijon mustard, and 1 teaspoon lemon juice. Mix well and go to town!

Wisconsin's Fried Cheese Curds

Folks in Wisconsin aren't afraid to get a little squeaky. (That's the sound heard when eating fresh cheese curds.) Cheese curds used to be a Wisconsin exclusive (although they've gained popularity around the country). During the cheese making process, milk is separated into curds and whey. Once the whey is drained, the randomly shaped curds are left to be salted and eaten as-is or to be formed and aged to make cheese. Battered and fried are a favorite way to eat them!

Serves 6

Ingredients

4 cups canola oil for frying

2 eggs

¼ cup milk

1 cup all-purpose flour

½ teaspoon salt

½ cup beer

1 pound cheese curds, broken apart

Preparation

1 In a deep skillet or deep fryer over medium-high heat, heat oil until hot but not smoking (375 degrees F).

2 Meanwhile, in a large bowl, whisk eggs and milk. Add flour, salt, and beer and whisk until smooth. Place about 8 cheese curds into batter, coating evenly. Remove curds with slotted spoon, shaking gently to remove excess batter.

3 Place curds into the oil and fry 1 to 2 minutes or until golden, turning once during cooking. Drain on a paper towel-lined platter. Repeat until all cheese curds are used. Serve piping hot.

Test Kitchen Tip: You can find cheese curds in the dairy case right alongside the other packaged cheeses. They come in a variety of flavors. Any flavor will work in this recipe, so pick your favorite.

No-Mess Buffalo Wings

Buffalo wings were born in Buffalo, New York, in a family-owned restaurant called Anchor Bar. They were created by Teressa Bellissimo in 1964 and have become so popular since then that there are now entire restaurants dedicated to selling chicken wings. While traditional Buffalo wings are deep-fried and then coated in Buffalo sauce, we found a way to make these just as traditional-tasting without all the mess. Don't forget the celery and blue cheese dipping sauce!

Serves 5

Ingredients

4 pounds chicken wings (see Note)

1 tablespoon vegetable oil

1-¼ teaspoons salt, divided

½ cup all-purpose flour

1 stick butter

¼ cup cayenne pepper sauce

1 tablespoon apple cider vinegar

¼ teaspoon hot sauce

¼ teaspoon garlic powder

Note: If you're using fresh wings, make sure to cut each wing in half so that you end up with a drumstick and a flat part. If they're frozen, they should already come split; just make sure you thaw them.

Preparation

1 Preheat oven to 425 degrees F. Coat 2 baking sheets with cooking spray.

2 In a large bowl, toss wings with oil and 1 teaspoon salt. Add flour and toss until wings are evenly coated. Place wings on baking sheets.

3 Bake 30 minutes, then turn wings over and bake 25 more minutes or until crispy.

4 Meanwhile, in a small saucepan over medium heat, melt butter. Stir in cayenne pepper sauce, vinegar, hot sauce, garlic powder, and remaining ¼ teaspoon salt. Bring to a boil, reduce heat to low, and simmer 5 minutes.

5 Place wings in a large bowl, add the sauce, and toss to coat. Serve immediately.

*Serving Suggestion: To make a homemade **Blue Cheese Dipping Sauce**, in a bowl simply combine ¾ cup sour cream, ¼ cup mayonnaise, 1-½ teaspoons white vinegar, 1 teaspoon vegetable oil, ¼ teaspoon salt, ¼ teaspoon black pepper, and 1 cup crumbled blue cheese. Mix well and refrigerate until ready to serve.*

Crispy-Fried Pickle Chips

Sometimes the window of opportunity can be pretty literal. At least that was the case for Bob Austin in 1960. His drive-in restaurant was located across the street from the Atkins Pickle Plant in Arkansas. After seeing it day after day from his window, he finally got an idea to try something new: deep fried dill pickles. As you may know, the idea took off and fried pickles are now a Southern favorite, especially when served with a creamy dressing.

Makes about 32

Ingredients

1 cup buttermilk ranch dressing

2 teaspoons hot sauce

½ cup buttermilk

½ teaspoon salt

¼ teaspoon black pepper

4 whole dill pickles, drained well, cut into ½-inch slices

1 cup cornmeal

½ cup all-purpose flour

1 teaspoon Cajun seasoning

1 teaspoon seafood seasoning

2 cups vegetable oil for frying

Preparation

1 To make dipping sauce, in a small bowl, combine ranch dressing and hot sauce; mix well and refrigerate until ready to serve.

2 In a shallow dish, combine buttermilk, salt, and pepper; mix well. Place pickles in buttermilk mixture and set aside.

3 In another shallow dish, combine cornmeal, flour, Cajun seasoning, and seafood seasoning; mix well.

4 In a deep skillet or deep fryer, heat oil until hot but not smoking (350 degrees F). Coat pickles evenly with cornmeal mixture, then fry in batches, 1 to 2 minutes per side or until golden and crispy. Place on a paper towel-lined platter.

5 Serve warm with the dipping sauce.

Taste-of-the-South Deviled Eggs

No one really knows when or where the first deviled egg was made. The idea dates all the way back to Ancient Rome and has been passed down through generations and cultures, changing every which way. Today, there are more ways to make deviled eggs than we have room to list. We decided to share just one favorite version that's enjoyed all over the South. These feature a traditional mayo base and plenty of sweet relish!

Makes 16

Ingredients

8 eggs

⅓ cup mayonnaise

1 teaspoon yellow mustard

2 tablespoons sweet pickle relish, plus extra for garnish, drained

¼ teaspoon salt

¼ teaspoon black pepper

Diced pimientos for garnish

Preparation

1 Place eggs in a soup pot and add just enough cold water to cover. Bring to a boil over high heat. When water begins to boil, remove pot from heat, cover, and let sit 18 minutes.

2 Drain the eggs and run cold water over them. Add some ice cubes to the water and let sit 5 to 10 minutes or until cool.

3 Peel the eggs, slice in half lengthwise, and remove the egg yolks to a medium bowl; mash with a fork until smooth. Add mayonnaise, mustard, relish, salt, and pepper; mix well.

4 Fill the cavity of each egg white half with the yolk mixture. Garnish with extra relish and pimientos. Serve immediately or cover and chill until ready to serve.

St. Louis Toasted Ravioli

The Hill is St. Louis' Italian neighborhood and where all the stories about the origins of toasted ravioli (also known as "t-rav") come from. There are many claims about who came up with this appetizer, but no facts to support any of them. Instead, there is one generally agreed upon belief: toasted ravioli was an accident. Luckily, it was a tasty one. So why are they called "toasted" and not "fried"? We're not sure, but that's not stopping us from eating our fill of these!

Makes about 24

Ingredients

1 egg

2 tablespoons milk

¾ cup Italian-seasoned bread crumbs

¼ teaspoon salt

1 cup vegetable oil

½ (25-ounce) package frozen cheese ravioli, thawed

Parmesan cheese for sprinkling

1 cup marinara sauce, warmed

Preparation

1 In a medium bowl, mix egg and milk. In another bowl, combine bread crumbs and salt; mix well and set aside.

2 In a deep skillet over medium heat, heat oil until hot, but not smoking.

3 Meanwhile, dip ravioli, a few at a time, into egg mixture, then into bread crumbs, until evenly coated. Fry ravioli 1 to 2 minutes per side or until golden; drain on a paper towel-lined platter.

4 Sprinkle with Parmesan cheese and serve with marinara sauce for dipping.

Caprese Avocado Toast

In the last decade, avocado toast has really taken off. It's pretty much agreed on that it first became popular in a New York restaurant, but we thought we'd give our thanks to California for this one. You see, California produces 90% of the nation's avocado crop. The Hass avocado is a native fruit of the state! Without rich and creamy California avocados it'd be a lot harder to enjoy our avocado toast, including this one that's perfect for serving at your next get-together.

Makes about 20

Ingredients

1 (1-pound) French bread, cut at an angle into ½-inch slices

3 ripe avocados, pitted and peeled

3 teaspoons fresh lemon juice

¼ teaspoon salt

8 ounces fresh mozzarella, sliced and cut to fit bread, if necessary

1 cup grape tomatoes, quartered

¼ cup basil leaves, slivered

Coarse black pepper for sprinkling

Balsamic glaze for drizzling

Preparation

1 Preheat oven to 375 degrees F. Coat a baking sheet with cooking spray. Place bread slices on baking sheet and bake 5 to 8 minutes or until lightly toasted.

2 Meanwhile, in a medium bowl, mash avocados with lemon juice and salt leaving mixture slightly chunky.

3 Spread avocado mixture evenly over bread slices, top with mozzarella slices, tomato, and basil. Sprinkle with pepper and drizzle with balsamic glaze. Serve immediately.

Test Kitchen Tips: *To make this really good, you want to make sure the avocados are ripe. That's what makes this so delicious. And if you are not familiar with balsamic glaze, it's simply balsamic vinegar that's been reduced. You can find this along with all the other vinegars at the market.*

The Ocean State's Clams Casino

Legend has it that Julius Keller invented this dish in the early 20th century while he was working at the Narragansett Pier Casino in Rhode Island. A wealthy guest requested clams for lunch, but didn't say how she wanted them prepared, so Keller decided to come up with something on his own. Named in honor of the restaurant he served, this decadent seafood appetizer was received with lots of praise. Set this one out for your guests and you'll be sure to impress them all.

Makes 24

Ingredients

4 slices bacon, finely chopped

½ stick butter

⅓ cup finely chopped onion

⅓ cup finely chopped red bell pepper

1 clove garlic, minced

¾ cup plain bread crumbs

1 tablespoon chopped fresh parsley

24 littleneck clams

Preparation

1 In a large skillet over medium heat, cook chopped bacon 5 to 7 minutes or until crispy, stirring occasionally. Add butter and heat until melted. Add onion, bell pepper, and garlic, and cook 3 to 5 minutes or until tender. Remove from heat and stir in bread crumbs and parsley; mix well and set aside.

2 Preheat oven to 400 degrees F.

3 Meanwhile, in a soup pot, bring 2 inches of water to a boil. Place the clams in water and cover. Steam the clams 5 to 8 minutes or until they open. Remove clams from pot, and discard any clams that do not open.

4 Remove the top shell of each and discard, leaving the clam in the bottom half of the shell. Spoon the bread crumb mixture evenly over the clams, filling each shell. Place on a baking sheet. Bake 10 to 12 minutes or until light golden.

Serving Suggestion: *To keep these warm and to make a fun presentation, serve these on a bed of hot sea or kosher salt, as shown. To warm the salt, place about 3 cups of salt in a 9- x 13-inch baking dish, and heat when the clams are in the oven.*

High Roller's Shrimp Cocktail

When it comes to extravagance, one city comes to mind before most: Las Vegas. The city is well known for its wide array of casinos, live entertainment venues, and buffets, among other things. And what's more fitting for an extravagant city than an extravagant appetizer like shrimp cocktail? In 1959, a hotel in the city even became famous for being the first to serve a fifty cent shrimp cocktail. As you can imagine, the appetizer quickly became a Vegas favorite.

Serves 5

Ingredients

COCKTAIL SAUCE

1 cup ketchup

1 tablespoon prepared horseradish, drained

½ teaspoon Worcestershire sauce

2 dashes hot sauce

10 cups cold water

2 celery stalks, quartered

1 large onion, quartered

3 cloves garlic, cut in half

1 lemon, cut in half

5 sprigs fresh thyme

2 bay leaves

1 tablespoon salt

1 pound raw, extra-large shrimp in shell

Preparation

1. To make Cocktail Sauce, in a small bowl, combine ketchup, horseradish, Worcestershire sauce, and hot sauce; mix well. Cover and refrigerate until ready to serve.

2. In a large pot over high heat, combine water, celery, onion, garlic, lemon, thyme, bay leaves, and salt; bring to a boil. Reduce heat to low and simmer 20 minutes, partially covering the pot.

3. Place shrimp in the seasoned water and turn off heat. Allow to poach 2 to 3 minutes or until shrimp turn pink, stirring once. Drain well and let cool. Peel shrimp, leaving tails on. Refrigerate until chilled. Serve with the homemade Cocktail Sauce.

Hot & Cheesy Hanky Pankies

What's gooey, cheesy, meaty, and ready to party? A hanky pankie! This party-style appetizer is a must-have in Cincinnati, where you'll see it included in the spread of practically every get-together. Outside of Cincinnati, it's popular in Missouri, where it's known as "Rye Pizza," and in Kentucky, where it's a popular menu item for Kentucky Derby parties. We've even heard that some people refer to this as "S.O.S.," but we won't get into that now. One thing's for sure, everyone loves these!

Makes about 18

Ingredients

½ pound ground beef

½ pound bulk Italian sausage, casing removed

3 tablespoons minced onion

8 ounces pasteurized cheese product, cut into chunks (see Tip)

½ teaspoon garlic powder

¼ teaspoon black pepper

1 (16-ounce) package cocktail rye bread

Preparation

1 Preheat oven to broil.

2 In a large skillet over medium-high heat, cook ground beef, sausage, and onion 6 to 8 minutes or until browned, breaking apart until crumbly. Drain excess liquid. Stir in cheese, garlic powder and pepper, and heat until cheese is melted.

3 Spread mixture generously onto rye bread slices and place on a rimmed baking sheet. (You'll probably have some leftover bread, so pop it into the freezer to save for another use.)

4 Broil for 3 to 4 minutes or until the cheesy mixture starts to bubble. Serve immediately.

Test Kitchen Tip: *We tested this with Velveeta®, but feel free to use whatever brand you like..*

Castroville's Stuffed Artichokes

The "Artichoke Center of the World" is located in Castroville, a little community in Monterey County, California. It's where most of the artichokes that are grown in the U.S. come from. It's also the home of the annual Castroville Artichoke Food & Wine Festival, which began in 1959. Fair visitors can take field tours, learn tasty ways to prepare artichokes, make artichoke art, and more! It's no wonder California named the artichoke its official state vegetable.

Makes 4

Ingredients

4 large artichokes, trimmed

¼ teaspoon salt

4 tablespoons olive oil, divided

½ stick butter

½ cup finely chopped onion

2 teaspoons minced garlic

1 cup Italian-flavored bread crumbs

1 tablespoon grated Parmesan cheese

¼ teaspoon black pepper

Preparation

1   In a large soup pot over high heat, place artichokes in enough water to cover them halfway and add salt. Bring to a boil, cover, and reduce heat to low. Cook 30 to 35 minutes or until artichokes are tender. (You'll know it's tender when you can easily pull out a leaf.)

2   Remove artichokes from water and drain upside down. Place right-side up in an 8-inch square baking dish; set aside.

3   Preheat oven to 375 degrees F.

4   To make stuffing mixture, in a skillet over medium heat, heat 3 tablespoons oil and the butter. Add onion and garlic, and cook 5 minutes or until onion is tender. Remove from heat and add in bread crumbs, cheese, and pepper; mix well.

5   Spread artichoke leaves apart and pack the stuffing between the leaves, as shown. Drizzle remaining oil over artichokes. Cover with aluminum foil and bake 15 to 20 minutes or until hot. Serve immediately.

Test Kitchen Tip: *Wondering how to get your artichokes ready for cooking? Just rinse in cold water, and use a sharp knife to simply trim off about an inch from both the top and the stem. Then, using kitchen shears, trim the pointy tips from each leaf.*

New England Clam Dip

A TV commercial advertising cream cheese first made this dip famous in the 1950s. In fact, it made it so famous that canned clams were sold out at grocery stores all across the country just a couple of days after it aired. Today, this dip is just as loved, particularly on bright summer days. The best part about it is you don't have to go clam digging, like they do in New England, to enjoy this creamy dip.

Makes about 1-½ cups

Ingredients

1 (8-ounce) package cream cheese, softened

2 tablespoons sour cream

2 (6.5-ounce) cans minced clams, drained

1 tablespoon chopped fresh parsley

2 teaspoons Worcestershire sauce

1 teaspoon lemon juice

1 teaspoon hot sauce

½ teaspoon seafood seasoning (see note)

½ teaspoon garlic powder

¼ teaspoon onion powder

¼ teaspoon black pepper

Preparation

1 In a medium bowl, combine all ingredients until thoroughly mixed. Refrigerate at least 1 hour or until ready to serve.

Note: We tested this with Old Bay® seafood seasoning.

Serving Suggestion: Although this is good enough to eat by the spoonful, we recommend serving it with some crackers and cut-up fresh veggies.

Crowd-Pleasing Pimento Spread

We've got some shocking news for you: pimento cheese did not originate in the South. Its long history begins in New York, where cream cheese was invented, and at a time when Spanish pimento peppers had become popular. Back then, it was considered a fancy food. When farmers in Georgia learned to grow the peppers, folks everywhere cheered. Pimento cheese became an everyday favorite, and Southerners made it a household staple. It's a real crowd-pleaser!

Makes about 2 cups

Ingredients

- 1 (8-ounce) package cream cheese, softened
- ¼ cup mayonnaise
- ½ stick butter, softened
- ¼ teaspoon sugar
- 1 teaspoon garlic powder
- ¼ teaspoon salt
- ⅛ teaspoon cayenne pepper
- 2 cups shredded sharp cheddar cheese
- 1 (4-ounce) jar chopped pimentos, drained
- ½ cup chopped pecans

Preparation

1 In a large bowl with an electric mixer, beat cream cheese, mayonnaise, butter, sugar, garlic powder, salt, and cayenne pepper until creamy. Add cheddar cheese, pimientos, and pecans and mix until thoroughly blended.

2 Place mixture in a bowl, cover, and refrigerate 1 hour or until ready to serve.

Serving Suggestion: *Let the party begin by serving this up with butter crackers and some cut-up fresh veggies. And yes, this also makes the ultimate Southern sandwich spread.*

We're not horsin' around when we say that the drive to the Kentucky Derby is magical. Just look at that scenery!

There are few things as relaxing as taking in the Hawaiian sunset from a hammock on the beach, especially after digging into some huli chicken (page 108) - ahh.

Nothing is more peaceful than driving up the coast and discovering great bed and breakfasts. We found that they have some of the best food!

Howard had a good time getting to know "Mr. Lobster" in New England. After a quick dip in the pool (of melted butter, that is), Mr. Lobster magically disappeared!

On our drive down Route 40 into Nashville, it was hard not to start drooling just thinking about all the great food we would soon be eating!

Simple Soups
& Sandwiches

Maryland Crab Soup

Do you ever throw things into a pot and hope for the best? That's sort of what the Native Americans did way back when, when they would toss their hunt or catch of the day into a pot of boiling water. If you've ever been to a crab boil, you might realize we're still doing this today. In fact, that's where this soup got its beginnings, and traditional recipes call for the leftover liquid of the boil to be used as a base.

Makes 6 cups

Ingredients

1 tablespoon vegetable oil

2 carrots, peeled and diced

1 stalk celery, chopped

½ cup chopped onion

4 cups water

1 (28-ounce) can whole peeled plum tomatoes, broken up

1-½ cups frozen lima beans

1 cup frozen corn

2 tablespoons seafood seasoning

2 tablespoons Worcestershire sauce

½ teaspoon salt

¼ teaspoon black pepper

1 pound refrigerated jumbo lump crabmeat

Preparation

1 In a soup pot over medium-high heat, heat oil until hot. Sauté carrot, celery, and onion 5 minutes. Add remaining ingredients except crabmeat and bring to a boil.

2 Reduce heat to low and simmer 25 minutes, stirring occasionally. Stir in crabmeat and heat 15 additional minutes.

Test Kitchen Tip: *You can find the crab right at the seafood counter in cans or plastic containers. When you're ready to use it, it's a good idea to pick through it just to make sure that all the shells and cartilage have been removed.*

Wild Rice & Turkey Soup

Wild rice grows in the lakes and marshes of northern Minnesota. It's harvested every fall and celebrated with an annual Wild Rice Festival. Traditionally, wild rice has been harvested by hand with the use of canoes and special tools. While more modern methods of harvesting are available today, Minnesotans still value and keep their traditional ways. The grain is used in many recipes and has a delicious, earthy taste to it. We really like the heartiness it adds to this soup!

Makes 8 cups

Ingredients

1 (6-ounce) package long grain and wild rice mix

½ stick butter

1 carrot, peeled and sliced

1 celery stalk, sliced

1-½ cups sliced fresh mushrooms

4 cups chicken broth

¼ teaspoon black pepper

1 cup half-and-half

2 cups chopped cooked turkey (see Tip)

Preparation

1 Prepare rice according to package directions, omitting butter or oil. (You'll be adding butter in the next step.)

2 In a soup pot over medium-high heat, melt butter; cook carrot and celery 5 minutes. Add mushrooms and cook 3 additional minutes, stirring occasionally. Add broth and pepper; bring to a boil. Reduce heat to medium-low and simmer 10 minutes.

3 Stir in half-and-half, the cooked rice, and turkey, and cook 8 minutes or until heated through.

Test Kitchen Tip: *This is a great way to use up leftover cooked turkey, but if you don't have any you can always use thick-sliced deli turkey or even a cut-up rotisserie chicken.*

New England Clam Chowder

In Boston, where this soup is considered a classic, they call this "chowdah," and it's pure comfort in a bowl. While some states go for the red tomato-based broth, in New England it's all about the thick and creamy, white broth loaded with plenty of potatoes and clams. A great place to try it is at the historic Union Oyster House in Boston, which is one of the oldest restaurants in the U.S. If you can't travel there don't worry, ours is just as good!

Makes 4 cups

Ingredients

1 tablespoon vegetable oil

½ cup chopped celery

¼ cup finely chopped onion

2 (10-ounce) cans whole baby clams, not drained

2 (8-ounce) bottles clam juice

1 large potato, peeled and diced

½ teaspoon dried thyme leaf

½ teaspoon salt

¼ teaspoon black pepper

3 tablespoons all-purpose flour

2 cups (1 pint) half-and-half, divided

1 tablespoon chopped fresh parsley

Preparation

1 In a soup pot over medium heat, heat oil until hot; sauté celery and onion 5 to 7 minutes or until tender. Add clams, clam juice, potato, thyme, salt, and pepper.

2 Cover and bring to a boil. Cook 10 to 12 minutes or until potatoes are tender.

3 In a small bowl, whisk flour and ½ cup half-and-half; slowly whisk into the soup. Add remaining 1-½ cups half-and-half and the parsley; cook 5 minutes or until thickened, stirring frequently.

Serving Suggestion: To add a smoky touch, top each bowl with some crumbled bacon. Oh, and don't forget the oyster crackers!

Colonial Virginia's Creamy Peanut Soup

Peanuts have quite a history in the United States, especially down in the South. One place to learn about how peanuts became so popular is at Colonial Williamsburg in Virginia. There, you can dine at the King's Arms Tavern and order a bowl of creamy peanut soup. Of course, now that you have this recipe, you can make it any time you get a craving. Just be warned, this soup is extra-rich and highly addictive!

Makes 8 cups

Ingredients

½ stick butter

½ cup chopped onion

2 celery stalks, chopped

3 tablespoons all-purpose flour

8 cups chicken broth

2 cups smooth peanut butter

1 cup heavy cream

Preparation

1 In a soup pot over medium-high heat, melt butter; cook onion and celery 5 minutes or until softened. Stir in flour and cook 1 minute. Slowly stir in broth and bring to a boil, stirring occasionally. Reduce heat to medium and cook 10 minutes or until slightly thickened.

2 Using a fine mesh strainer, strain broth into a large bowl, discarding onion and celery. Return broth to pot. Add peanut butter and heavy cream; whisk until smooth. Heat over low heat 5 minutes or until hot, stirring occasionally.

Serving Suggestion: We like to sprinkle a few chopped peanuts over each bowl before digging in.

Southwestern Tortilla Soup

There's not much that's known about the origins of tortilla soup, except that most sources agree that it comes from Mexico. How it came into and became popular in the U.S. is kind of a mystery. Nowadays, it's the soup of choice in some regions of the country, like the Southwest. You'll just as easily see it on the menu of your favorite restaurant as you would on the shelves at your market. Everyone's version is slightly different, so don't be afraid to experiment!

Makes 8 cups

Ingredients

1 tablespoon vegetable oil

1 pound boneless, skinless chicken breasts, cut into ½-inch chunks

1 red bell pepper, chopped

3 cloves garlic, minced

6 cups chicken broth

2 cups frozen corn

½ cup salsa

½ teaspoon chili powder

½ teaspoon ground cumin

2 tablespoons chopped fresh cilantro

4 cups tortilla chips

Preparation

1 In a soup pot over medium heat, heat oil until hot. Add chicken, bell pepper, and garlic, and cook 5 minutes, stirring frequently.

2 Add chicken broth, corn, salsa, chili powder, and cumin; bring to a boil. Reduce heat to low and simmer 10 minutes or until chicken is no longer pink.

3 Stir in cilantro and serve with tortilla chips on the side or crush them and stir them into the soup so that they can soak in all the goodness.

Serving Suggestion: *Right before digging in, we like to add a dollop of sour cream to really get the fiesta started!*

Wisconsin Brats & Cheesy Beer Soup

This is basically the ultimate Wisconsin soup. After all, it's made with three ingredients that are really important to the folks there: brats, beer, and cheese. Their love of brats comes from German traditions while their love of beer comes from a long history of breweries. As for the cheese? Well, you don't get to be known as "America's Dairyland" for nothing! Wisconsin produces more cheese than any other state. Now get ready to slurp up every last bit of this one!

Makes 7 cups

Ingredients

1 tablespoon vegetable oil

3 bratwursts

½ stick butter

¼ cup finely chopped onion

⅓ cup all-purpose flour

2 cups chicken broth

1 cup milk

1 teaspoon Worcestershire sauce

3 cups shredded cheddar cheese

1 cup beer

1 teaspoon hot sauce

Preparation

1 In a medium skillet over medium heat, heat oil until hot. Cook bratwursts 10 to 12 minutes or until browned on all sides and no longer pink in center, turning occasionally. Let cool slightly before cutting into ½-inch slices. Set aside.

2 In a soup pot over medium heat, melt butter. Add onion and cook 5 minutes or until softened. Stir in flour and cook 1 minute. Add broth, milk, and Worcestershire sauce; bring to a boil, then cook 5 minutes or until mixture has thickened.

3 Add cheese and cook 1 to 2 minutes or until cheese is melted. Add beer, hot sauce, and sliced bratwurst, and cook 5 minutes or until heated through.

Test Kitchen Tip: *Sure you can use pre-shredded cheese, but to get a smoother sauce we suggest shredding your own and adding it in slowly.*

Buffalo's Beef on Weck

Beef on weck is almost exclusive to Buffalo, New York. It was created by Joe Gohn, owner of a hotel and tavern called The Delaware House in the early 1900s. Like any good businessman, Joe wanted to offer his patrons something tasty to eat, and something that would make them want to drink more beer. With the help of his German baker, he created this roast beef sandwich on kummelweck, a type of Kaiser roll with caraway seeds and salt added. It was a hit!

Serves 4

Ingredients

1 cup beef broth

4 Kaiser rolls

2 teaspoons kosher salt

2 teaspoons caraway seeds

1 pound thinly sliced deli roast beef

2 tablespoons prepared horseradish

Preparation

1 Preheat oven to 350 degrees F.

2 In a small saucepan over medium heat, bring broth to a gentle boil.

3 Meanwhile, place rolls on baking sheet and lightly brush tops with water. Sprinkle the top of the rolls evenly with salt and caraway seeds. Bake 5 minutes or until lightly toasted. Let rolls cool slightly, then cut in half.

4 Place roast beef evenly over the bottom of the rolls, then top with horseradish. Drizzle hot broth over the meat. Dip the cut side of the top of the roll into broth, then place top on sandwich and serve.

Springfield's Horseshoe Sandwiches

Springfield, Illinois' signature Horseshoe Sandwich was created in the 1920s by Joe Schweska. Following his wife's suggestion, Joe came up with an open-faced sandwich to add to the menu of the hotel restaurant he worked at. It was given the name "Horseshoe" because the ham was cut around the bone, which gave it a horseshoe shape. The fries are considered to be the "nails" of the horseshoe. This sandwich is a taste bud-pleasin' dream come true.

Serves 2

Ingredients

½ (16-ounce) bag frozen thin-cut French fries

½ cup beer

2 egg yolks

4 tablespoons butter, divided

3 cups shredded sharp cheddar cheese

1 teaspoon Worcestershire sauce

¼ teaspoon dry mustard

¼ teaspoon salt

¼ teaspoon cayenne pepper

¼ teaspoon black pepper

1 pound boneless ham steak, cut into 4 pieces

4 slices home-style white bread, toasted

Chives for garnish (optional)

Preparation

1 Prepare French fries according to package directions.

2 Meanwhile, in a small bowl, combine beer and egg yolks; mix well.

3 In a saucepan over medium heat, melt 3 tablespoons butter and the cheese, stirring constantly. Stir in Worcestershire sauce, dry mustard, salt, cayenne pepper, and black pepper. Gradually add beer mixture, stirring constantly. Cook 3 to 5 minutes or until mixture thickens. Remove from heat and cover to keep warm.

4 Meanwhile, in a large skillet over medium-high heat, melt remaining 1 tablespoon butter; sauté ham 6 to 8 minutes or until edges are browned. Arrange toast on plates, top with ham and French fries (yes, the fries go on the sandwich!), then spoon on the cheese sauce, and sprinkle with chives, if desired. Serve immediately.

The Ultimate Grilled Reuben

Here's a question that'll help stir up a friendly debate: Where was the first reuben sandwich created? Some of you might say New York, where the reuben is undoubtedly a deli favorite, while others might say Nebraska, because...well, there's a pretty good story that comes from there too. Both involve a real-life "Reuben," who was either the creator of the sandwich (New York) or the recipient (Nebraska). It doesn't matter. We're just thankful this sandwich is around!

Serves 6

Ingredients

1 (3- to 4-pound) raw corned beef, cooked according to package directions

12 slices rye bread

1 cup Russian dressing

1 (16-ounce) package refrigerated sauerkraut, well drained

12 slices Swiss cheese

6 tablespoons butter, softened

Preparation

1 Once the corned beef is cooked until tender, allow to cool slightly and cut ¼-inch slices across the grain.

2 Evenly spread each slice of bread with Russian dressing. Evenly top 6 slices of bread with sauerkraut, sliced corned beef, and 2 slices of Swiss cheese. Top with remaining bread slices. Spread butter on both sides of the sandwiches.

3 In a skillet or on a griddle over medium heat, cook in batches until golden on both sides and cheese is melted.

Test Kitchen Tip: *There are a couple of different ways to cook corned beef. If you've got time, try making it in your slow cooker, so it cooks all day and it's nice and tender by the time you get home. If you're pressed for time, then dig out the pressure cooker!*

Kentucky Hot Browns

The Hot Brown sandwich was created in Louisville, Kentucky at the Brown Hotel. During the 1920s, late-night dance parties were pretty popular, and the Brown Hotel was one of the many places where folks could go for a good time. They would often take a break and order food, which was traditionally ham and eggs. In 1926, Chef Fred K. Schmidt had the idea to offer something new, an open-faced turkey sandwich topped with bacon and Mornay sauce. History was made.

Serves 4

Ingredients

1 tablespoon butter

1 tablespoon all-purpose flour

1 cup heavy cream

½ cup grated Romano cheese

⅛ teaspoon ground nutmeg

¼ teaspoon salt

⅛ teaspoon black pepper

4 slices home-style white bread, toasted

½ pound thinly sliced deli turkey breast

2 plum tomatoes, thinly sliced

8 slices crispy cooked bacon

Preparation

1 To make Mornay sauce, in a small saucepan over medium heat, melt butter. Whisk in flour and cook 1 minute, stirring occasionally. Gradually add cream and whisk until smooth and mixture begins to thicken. Stir in cheese, nutmeg, salt, and pepper, and heat until smooth and creamy. Set aside.

2 Preheat oven to broil. Place toasted bread on a baking sheet. (Or you can make these in individual baking dishes, like we did.) Top each slice evenly with a layer of turkey. Spoon Mornay sauce over turkey, top with tomato slices, and bacon strips. Broil 2 to 3 minutes or until Mornay sauce is light golden. Serve immediately.

Serving Suggestion: Since you can never have too much cheese, we suggest sprinkling with some extra Romano cheese right before serving.

Pressed Cuban Sandwiches

Two Florida cities claim this sandwich as their own: Tampa and Miami. The sandwich was created by Cuban immigrants, hence the name. While there are a few accepted variations, traditional versions usually agree that all Cuban sandwiches must have mustard, roasted pork, and pickles. They're also typically pressed in a plancha, which is a Cuban sandwich press. This makes all of the layers of meat and cheese fuse together, resulting in one really tasty sandwich.

Serves 4

Ingredients

¼ cup yellow mustard

1 loaf Cuban bread, sliced in half horizontally

8 long dill pickle slices

½ pound thinly sliced deli baked ham

½ pound thinly sliced deli roast pork

8 slices Swiss cheese

2 tablespoons butter, softened

Preparation

1 Spread mustard evenly on both cut sides of bread. Layer bottom half with pickles, ham, pork, and cheese. Replace top half of bread and cut into 4 sandwiches.

2 Spread butter on top and bottom of sandwiches and grill on a hot panini press or a grill pan (see note) until cheese is melted and bread is golden. Slice in half and serve immediately.

So Many Options: No Cuban bread? No problem! You can always use Italian or French bread instead. And if you don't have a panini press, you can always give your sandwiches that pressed look and taste by placing them on a grill pan and placing a cookie sheet and some heavy cans over them.

Open-Wide "BPT" Sandwiches

Don't worry about your pork tenderloin hanging out over your bun - it's supposed to do that! "BPT" is short for "breaded pork tenderloin" and it refers to the sandwich that is famous all over the Midwest, but especially in Indiana where it first appeared. The pork tenderloin is the star of this sandwich. It's sometimes breaded, sometimes battered, but always cooked to juicy perfection. Top it with all your favorite sandwich toppings and open wide!

Serves 6

Ingredients

2 pounds pork tenderloin or center-cut boneless pork loin, cut into 6 equal pieces

2 cups buttermilk

2 eggs

1 teaspoon garlic powder

1 cup all-purpose flour

1 teaspoon salt

½ teaspoon black pepper

2 sleeves saltine crackers, crushed (about 80)

½ teaspoon cayenne pepper

⅓ cup peanut oil

6 soft hamburger buns, split

1-½ cups shredded iceberg lettuce

2 tomatoes, sliced

12 long dill pickle slices

½ red onion, thinly sliced

Preparation

1 Slice each pork piece horizontally almost in half, stopping 1 inch from other side. Open like a book. Place pork between 2 sheets of wax paper and pound to ¼-inch thickness.

2 In a shallow dish, whisk buttermilk, eggs, and garlic powder. In another shallow dish, combine flour, salt, and black pepper; mix well. In a third shallow dish, place cracker crumbs and cayenne pepper; mix well. Dip pork in buttermilk mixture, shaking off excess. Dredge pork in flour mixture, then dip again in buttermilk mixture. Place in cracker mixture, coating evenly on both sides.

3 In a large skillet over medium-high heat, heat oil until hot. Sauté pork in batches 3 to 4 minutes per side or until golden brown and cooked through. Place on a paper towel-lined platter.

4 Place pork on buns and top with lettuce, tomato, pickles, and onion.

Serving Suggestion: Don't forget to add your favorite condiments like mayo, mustard, or ketchup!

Shrimp Po' Boys

One widely accepted legend claims that this sandwich was originally named after the "poor boys" who lost their jobs during the transit strikes of the late 1920s and early 1930s. The Martin brothers, who owned a restaurant in New Orleans and were former streetcar conductors, offered free sandwiches to the strikers. The sandwiches were made on specially designed loaves of French bread and filled with everything from shrimp and oysters to crab, catfish, and more.

Serves 4

Ingredients

- ⅓ cup all-purpose flour
- 1 tablespoon Creole seasoning
- 2 eggs
- 1 cup panko bread crumbs
- 2 cups vegetable oil
- 1 pound large shrimp, peeled and deveined, with tails removed
- ½ stick butter, melted
- 1 teaspoon minced garlic
- 4 French rolls, split
- 2 cups shredded iceberg lettuce
- 1 large tomato, sliced thin
- ½ cup store-bought remoulade sauce

Preparation

1 In a shallow dish, combine flour and Creole seasoning; mix well. In another shallow dish, beat eggs. Place bread crumbs in a third shallow dish.

2 In a large deep skillet over medium heat, heat oil until hot, but not smoking. Coat shrimp evenly in flour mixture, then egg, and then in bread crumbs. Place in oil and fry 3 to 4 minutes or until golden, turning once during cooking. Remove to a paper towel-lined platter.

3 Preheat oven to 375 degrees F. In a small bowl, combine butter and garlic. Brush mixture evenly on cut-side of rolls and place open-faced on baking sheet. Bake 3 to 5 minutes or until toasted.

4 Top rolls with lettuce, tomato, and shrimp, then drizzle with remoulade sauce.

Test Kitchen Tip: *If you'd like to make your own* **Remoulade Sauce** *all you have to do is, in a bowl, combine ⅔ cup mayonnaise, ⅓ cup Dijon mustard, 1 minced scallion, 1 tablespoon capers, and ½ teaspoon Worcestershire sauce. Mix well, and it's ready to drizzle on.*

Maine Lobster Rolls

When we say Maine, you say...lobster? Lobstermen have been hand-harvesting lobsters in Maine since way back in the 1600s. Today, the state produces more lobsters than anywhere else in the world! And folks are eating it every which way. One delicious way to enjoy this tasty crustacean is inside a toasted hot dog roll. While there is some debate about its true origins (some say it was invented in Connecticut!), no one can argue with Maine's love for all things lobster.

Serves 2

Ingredients

1 (1 to 1-¼-pound) fresh lobster

¼ cup mayonnaise

½ cup chopped celery

1 tablespoon lemon juice

¼ teaspoon salt

¼ teaspoon black pepper

2 tablespoons butter, melted

4 New England-style top-split hotdog rolls

Preparation

1 Fill a soup pot with water about ¾ of the way full and bring to a boil over high heat. Place live lobster into the pot, claws first, and return to a boil. Cook 15 to 20 minutes or until lobster turns bright red. Carefully remove from pot and let cool. Using a seafood cracker, remove meat from lobster and cut into chunks. (Be careful, the lobster shells can be sharp.)

2 In a medium bowl, combine mayonnaise, celery, lemon juice, salt, and pepper; mix well. Stir in lobster and refrigerate until ready to use.

3 Brush butter on outside of rolls and lightly toast. Fill rolls evenly with lobster mixture and serve.

Test Kitchen Tip: When making these, don't overdo it with the mayo. The lobster should be lightly dressed and not smothered in dressing. After all, it's all about the fresh lobster meat!

Philly Cheesesteak Sandwiches

It all started when a hot dog vendor by the name of Pat Olivieri decided to throw some beef on his grill in 1930. The rest, as they say, is history. Today, the Philly Cheesesteak is one of the most debated sandwiches in the country. From the way the meat is chopped to the kind of cheese used, everyone's got their favorite way. If you were ordering this sandwich in one of Philly's famous spots, you'd ask for "one-whiz-wit" (one cheesesteak, with Cheese Whiz®, and onions).

Serves 4

Ingredients

1 (1-pound) rib eye steak

3 tablespoons vegetable oil

2 onions, thinly sliced

½ teaspoon salt

½ teaspoon black pepper

4 hoagie rolls, split

1 (8-ounce) jar cheese dip, melted

Preparation

1 Place steak in freezer for about 1 hour to firm up.

2 In a large skillet over medium-high heat, heat oil until hot. Add onions, and sauté 10 to 12 minutes or until tender. Transfer to a bowl and set aside.

3 Meanwhile, remove steak from freezer. The steak should be firm, but not frozen solid. Cut into thin slices. Add beef to skillet and sprinkle with salt and pepper; sauté 3 to 5 minutes or until no pink remains in beef.

4 Place steak on hoagie rolls, top with onions, and drizzle with melted cheese; serve immediately.

Test Kitchen Tip: *Freezing the steak slightly makes it easier to cut into thin slices.*

Ever wonder what happens when Kelly, Patty, and Howard visit the local farmer's market? Here's a clue. Check out our inspired recipe on page 188.

There's so much to look at and explore at the Pike Place Market in Seattle, WA. You'll see "flying" fresh fish, endless produce, and baked goods galore.

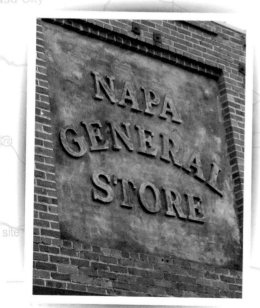

Taping shows on the road can be fun and a little challenging. If I'd gotten any closer to the fence, I might have had a run-in with the Secret Service!

After a hot air balloon ride over the Napa Valley, we had brunch at the Napa General Store. Don't let the name fool ya - there's lots of good local fare and drink found here.

While on our way to visit our friends at Wheel of Fortune® in Culver City, CA, we ran across the most colorful farmer's market ever.

Pleasing Poultry

Nashville's Hot Chicken

Ever heard the proverb, "Hell hath no fury like a woman scorned"? If you have, then you'll understand why one of Thornton Prince's lovers finally got tired of his womanizing ways and decided to get her revenge. She did this by surprising him with an extra-spicy version of his favorite food - fried chicken. Unfortunately, her plan backfired. Thornton loved it so much he opened up Prince's Hot Chicken Shack in Nashville. Fortunately for all of us, the spicy chicken was a hit.

Serves 4

Ingredients

1 (3-½ to 4-pound) chicken, cut into 10 pieces (breasts cut in half)

2 tablespoons kosher salt, divided

2 teaspoons black pepper

1-½ cups all-purpose flour

2 eggs

1-½ cups buttermilk

1 tablespoon hot sauce

4 cups vegetable oil

1 tablespoon light brown sugar

1 teaspoon cayenne pepper

½ teaspoon chili powder

½ teaspoon paprika

½ teaspoon garlic powder

Preparation

1 In a large bowl, season chicken with 1 tablespoon salt and the black pepper; cover and refrigerate at least 2 hours.

2 In a large bowl, combine flour and remaining 1 tablespoon salt; mix well. In another large bowl, whisk eggs, buttermilk, and hot sauce. In a deep skillet over medium heat, heat oil until hot, but not smoking (about 325 degrees F). Pat chicken dry. Coat chicken evenly in flour mixture, then in buttermilk mixture, shaking off excess, then re-coat in flour mixture.

3 Fry chicken in batches 15 to 20 minutes or until golden brown and no longer pink inside, or it registers 165 degrees F with a meat thermometer, turning occasionally. Place chicken on a paper towel-lined platter. Reserve ½ cup of the frying oil.

4 In a medium bowl, whisk brown sugar, cayenne pepper, chili powder, paprika, garlic powder, and reserved frying oil. Generously brush fried chicken with oil mixture and serve.

Serving Suggestion: *In Nashville, hot chicken is traditionally served on a slice of white bread and topped with a couple of pickle slices. We love how the bread soaks up all the extra sauce!*

Little Italy's Chicken Parmesan

Italian-American neighborhoods exist all over the country, especially in major cities. Several of these neighborhoods have been given the nickname of "Little Italy" due to their rich Italian culture. In any of them, you're likely to find great Italian markets and restaurants that specialize in Italian food. One dish that's particularly popular is Chicken Parmesan. This breaded, fried, and smothered chicken dish is always good.

Serves 4

Ingredients

1 cup Italian bread crumbs

1 teaspoon garlic powder

2 eggs

1 tablespoon water

4 boneless, skinless chicken breasts, flattened to ¼-inch thickness

Salt and pepper for sprinkling

¼ cup olive oil

2 cups spaghetti sauce

8 slices mozzarella cheese

Preparation

1 Preheat oven to 375 degrees F. Coat a baking sheet with cooking spray.

2 In a shallow dish, combine bread crumbs and garlic powder. In another shallow dish, whisk eggs and water. Evenly sprinkle both sides of chicken with salt and pepper. In a large skillet over medium heat, heat oil until hot. Dip chicken in egg mixture, then in bread crumbs, coating evenly on both sides.

3 Sauté chicken 5 to 6 minutes or until golden brown, turning halfway through cooking. Remove to baking sheet.

4 Evenly spoon sauce over chicken, then top with cheese. Bake 8 to 10 minutes or until chicken is no longer pink in center and the cheese begins to turn golden.

Serving Suggestion: *To round out the meal, serve with a side of pasta and sauce, as well as some crispy garlic bread.*

Cornell Chicken

Dr. Robert C. Baker, a former poultry and food science professor at Cornell University, came up with this amazing chicken recipe. The secret is in the sauce. While it may sound simple, Dr. Baker found that these ingredients made for a mouthwatering marinade. The trick to making it really flavorful is in the basting. In his original recipe, this chicken is meant to be barbecued, but we've found that you can make it in your oven with the same tasty results!

Serves 4

Ingredients

1 (3-½ to 4-pound) chicken, cut into quarters

1 egg

½ cup vegetable oil

1 cup apple cider vinegar

2 teaspoons poultry seasoning

2 teaspoons kosher salt

¼ teaspoon black pepper

Preparation

1 Place chicken in a large resealable plastic bag. In a large bowl, whisk egg and oil until mixture becomes thick. Whisk in remaining ingredients. Pour mixture over chicken, seal bag, and toss to coat evenly. Refrigerate at least 3 hours or overnight.

2 When ready to cook, preheat oven to 375 degrees F. Coat a baking sheet with cooking spray. Place chicken on baking sheet and baste with some of the marinade from plastic bag.

3 Roast 1 to 1-¼ hours or until golden and no longer pink in center, basting chicken several times during only the first 45 minutes of cooking. Discard any remaining marinade.

So Many Options: *If you prefer to cook this on the grill, make sure you do so over indirect heat and flip it a few times. You can also roast this chicken in the oven and finish it off on the grill to give it some smoky goodness.*

Chicken & Sausage Jambalaya

For a one-pot meal that's frugal, filling, and flavorful, look no further than this Louisiana favorite. Jambalaya is a dish made with rice, meat, and veggies that's typically categorized as either "Cajun" or "Creole," depending on the order that the ingredients are cooked and whether tomatoes have been added in. There are many regional varieties of jambalaya, all of which have been influenced by the people of various cultures who came to New Orleans centuries ago.

Serves 6

Ingredients

¼ cup vegetable oil

1 cup chopped onion

1 green bell pepper, chopped

1 teaspoon salt

½ teaspoon cayenne pepper

½ pound andouille sausage, cut into ½-inch slices

1-½ pounds boneless chicken breasts and/or thighs, cut into 1-inch chunks

1-½ cups long grain white rice

1 bay leaf

3 cups water

Preparation

1 In a soup pot or Dutch oven over medium heat, heat oil until hot. Cook onion, bell pepper, salt, and cayenne pepper 8 to 10 minutes or until vegetables begin to brown. Add sausage and cook 5 minutes. Add chicken and cook 8 to 10 minutes or until chicken begins to brown.

2 Stir in rice, bay leaf, and water; cover and cook 20 to 25 minutes or until rice is tender and liquid has been absorbed. Remove bay leaf and serve.

So Many Options: You can adjust the heat to your liking by using mild or spicy andouille sausage. You can also increase or decrease the amount of cayenne pepper. Just remember, you can always add spice, but you can't take it out!

Sweet & Savory Chicken & Waffles

To understand the complete history of this dish you've got to break it down into two parts: fried chicken and waffles. Both came from different places at different times, but somehow found their way to one another in what we can only call sheer, tasty luck. The delicious duo, as we know it today, really made its name in the 1930s at a Harlem restaurant called the Wells Supper Club. Since then, this sweet and savory combo has been popularized from coast to coast.

Serves 5

Ingredients

CHICKEN TENDERS
1 cup self-rising flour

¾ teaspoon black pepper

2 eggs

¼ cup hot sauce

2 tablespoons water

10 chicken tenders

Salt for sprinkling

Garlic powder for sprinkling

2 cups vegetable oil

WAFFLES
2 cups all-purpose flour

2 tablespoons sugar

1 tablespoon baking powder

1 teaspoon salt

2 eggs

1-¾ cups milk

½ stick butter, melted

1 teaspoon vanilla extract

Syrup for drizzling

Preparation

1 In a shallow dish, combine self-rising flour and pepper; mix well. In another shallow dish, whisk 2 eggs, the hot sauce, and water. Sprinkle chicken evenly with salt and garlic powder.

2 In a large deep skillet over medium heat, heat oil until hot but not smoking. Dip chicken tenders in egg mixture, then in flour mixture, coating evenly. Fry chicken 8 to 10 minutes or until golden and no pink remains, turning once during cooking. Drain on a cooling rack, and cover to keep warm.

3 Preheat waffle maker. In a large bowl, combine 2 cups all-purpose flour, sugar, baking powder, and salt; mix well. In a medium bowl, whisk 2 eggs, the milk, butter, and vanilla. Pour egg mixture into flour mixture and stir until well combined. Coat waffle maker with cooking spray.

4 Pour about ½ cup batter onto waffle maker (this will vary a bit based on your waffle maker, so adjust accordingly). Cook 3 to 5 minutes or until golden and crisp. Remove waffle and repeat until all batter is used. Serve chicken on top of the waffles and drizzle with maple syrup.

Tried-and-True Brunswick Stew

On a town monument in Brunswick, Georgia you'll find a 25-gallon iron pot with an inscription that claims it was the pot used to make the first Brunswick Stew. But folks in Brunswick County, Virginia will shake their heads and say the first stew was made in their town in 1828 by a chef on a hunting trip. Luckily, this friendly rivalry hasn't stopped anyone from cooking this hearty Southern stew. And while wild game might be traditional, ours is a more modern preparation.

Serves 6

Ingredients

1 tablespoon vegetable oil

1 pound ground pork

1 cup chopped onions

3 cloves garlic, minced

3 cups chicken broth

1 (28-ounce) can crushed tomatoes

½ cup ketchup

1-½ cups frozen lima beans

1-½ cups frozen corn

1 teaspoon dried thyme leaf

¼ teaspoon cayenne pepper

1 teaspoon salt

½ teaspoon black pepper

3 cups shredded cooked rotisserie chicken

Preparation

1 In a soup pot or Dutch oven over medium-high heat, heat oil until hot. Sauté pork, onion, and garlic, breaking up the pork as it cooks, 8 to 10 minutes or until well browned.

2 Stir in remaining ingredients and bring to a boil. Reduce heat to low and simmer 30 to 35 minutes or until mixture has thickened. Dish up hearty bowls and grab a spoon.

Test Kitchen Tip: *No need to thaw the veggies, as they will thaw within minutes when you start cooking them.*

Kansas City Fried Chicken

Fried chicken has a long history, so instead of taking you all the way back, we're starting with the decade that really turned fried chicken into a phenomenon - the 1950s. It was during this time that fast food restaurants began selling fried chicken, making it easily available and affordable to folks. As you know, it was a success! Today, fried chicken is loved all over the country (not just in the South) and there are many regional variations, like this pan-fried version from Kansas City.

Serves 4

Ingredients

3 cups vegetable oil

½ cup milk

1 egg

1 (3- to 3-½-pound) chicken, cut into 8 pieces

1 cup all-purpose flour

1 teaspoon paprika

1 tablespoon salt

1 teaspoon black pepper

Preparation

1 In a large deep skillet over medium heat, heat oil until hot, but not smoking. (Make sure the oil does not fill the pan more than halfway up; if so, grab a deeper pan.)

2 In a large bowl, combine milk and egg; mix well. Add chicken, coating completely. In another large bowl, combine flour, paprika, salt, and pepper; mix well. Remove chicken from milk mixture and dredge it in flour mixture, coating completely. Then re-dip each piece in milk and flour mixtures.

3 Carefully place chicken in oil and cook 20 to 25 minutes or until coating is brown and chicken is no longer pink inside or it registers 165 degrees F with a meat thermometer. Drain on a cooling rack. Serve immediately

Test Kitchen Tip: If you want to make this ahead of time, go ahead! When you're ready to reheat and serve, just place the chicken on a baking sheet in a 300 degree oven for 20 to 30 minutes or until heated through.

Slippery Pot Pie

You're looking at the photo on the next page and you're thinking, "That's not a pot pie!" Well, it is! At least it's a version of one that's popular in Lancaster County, Pennsylvania. There, this thick, brothy, and chicken soup-like dish is a favorite comfort food. One of the most unique features of this pot pie is the big, square, "slippery noodles" that are added in. Cozy up to a bowl and enjoy every hearty bite, just like the Pennsylvania Dutch do.

Serves 5

Ingredients

10 cups water

1 (3- to 3-½-pound) chicken, cut into 8 pieces

1 large onion, cut into 1-inch chunks

2 carrots, cut into 1-inch chunks

2 celery stalks, cut into ½-inch chunks

1 tablespoon salt

½ teaspoon black pepper

5 white potatoes, peeled and cut into quarters

1 refrigerated rolled pie crust (from a 14.1-ounce box), cut into 2-inch squares

Preparation

1 In a soup pot over medium-high heat, combine water, chicken, onion, carrots, celery, salt, and pepper; bring to a boil. Cover, reduce heat to medium-low, and cook 1 hour. Remove chicken to a platter, then add potatoes to pot and cook 10 more minutes.

2 Meanwhile, remove bones and skin from chicken, and cut chicken into bite-sized pieces.

3 Add pie dough to pot, a couple of pieces at a time, so they don't stick together. Cover and cook 8 to 10 minutes or until dough is tender. Return chicken to pot and continue cooking until heated through. Dish up and dig in.

Test Kitchen Tip: *This will thicken up as it sits, so you may need to add additional water Also, we like to add a bit of chopped fresh parsley to the pot right before serving for even more great taste.*

Hawaii's Huli Chicken

Hawaii's got its own version of teriyaki chicken, and it's thanks to a man named Ernest Morgado. Ernest made his chicken famous by serving it at fundraisers and charitable events throughout Hawaii. Eventually, he began to sell bottles of the sweet and tangy, soy-based sauce that he would use to glaze his chicken. The sauce is considered a Hawaiian staple. The word "Huli" means "turn" in Hawaiian, and it refers to the process of "turning" the chicken to cook it evenly.

Serves 4

Ingredients

1 cup pineapple juice

½ cup soy sauce

½ cup ketchup

2 tablespoons sherry or red wine vinegar

½ cup light brown sugar

2 teaspoons ground ginger

1 tablespoon garlic powder

2 teaspoons paprika

1 teaspoon onion powder

1 teaspoon ground cumin

1 tablespoon kosher salt

½ teaspoon cayenne pepper

½ teaspoon black pepper

1 (2-½- to 3-pound) chicken, cut in half

Preparation

1 Preheat oven to 400 degrees F. Place wire baking rack on rimmed baking sheet and coat with cooking spray.

2 In a small saucepan over medium heat, combine pineapple juice, soy sauce, ketchup, sherry, brown sugar, and ginger; bring to a boil, reduce heat to low, and simmer 5 minutes or until mixture is thickened, stirring occasionally. Reserve ½ cup of this sauce for serving; you'll use the rest for basting.

3 In a small bowl, combine garlic powder, paprika, onion powder, cumin, salt, cayenne pepper, and black pepper; mix well. Coat chicken evenly with spice mixture and place on baking rack.

4 Roast chicken 1 hour or until no longer pink in center, turning each half over about every ten minutes. Brush with basting sauce every time you turn the halves over. Do not baste chicken during last 10 minutes of cooking. Discard remaining sauce used for basting, cut each half in half, and serve with reserved sauce.

Chicken Ramen Bowls

Although ramen noodles got their start in China, they were brought to the U.S. by the Japanese. The first instant ramen noodles were invented in Japan in 1958, but they didn't make it into the U.S. (California) until the 1970s. At first, they were considered a luxury food item, but they quickly became a budget-friendly staple. And, over the last decade, ramen has become really trendy, with hundreds of gourmet ramen restaurants popping up in major cities across the country.

Serves 4

Ingredients

2 boneless, skinless chicken breasts

Salt and pepper for sprinkling

2 teaspoons sesame oil

3 cloves garlic, minced

2 teaspoons minced fresh ginger

4 cups chicken broth

3 tablespoons soy sauce

1 cup sliced fresh mushrooms

2 (3-ounce) packages ramen noodles (seasoning packet discarded)

2 soft boiled eggs, cut in half (see Tip)

1 scallion, sliced

½ red bell pepper, thinly sliced

Preparation

1 Coat a grill pan or skillet with cooking spray. Sprinkle chicken evenly with salt and pepper. Over medium heat, heat grill pan and sauté chicken 10 to 12 minutes or until no pink remains in center, turning once during cooking. Cut into ½-inch slices and cover to keep warm.

2 Meanwhile, in a soup pot over medium heat, heat oil until hot. Add garlic and ginger and cook 2 minutes. Add broth and soy sauce; bring to a boil. Stir in mushrooms, reduce heat to low, and simmer 5 minutes. Add noodles and cook 3 to 5 minutes or until soft.

3 Divide noodles evenly into bowls, add broth mixture, and top with sliced chicken, half an egg, scallions, and bell pepper.

Test Kitchen Tip: *To make soft boiled eggs, fill a saucepan with enough water to cover eggs, and bring to a boil over medium-high heat. Cover saucepan, remove from heat, and let sit 9 minutes. Drain eggs and cover with ice cubes. Let sit 5 minutes, then carefully peel.*

Seattle's Teriyaki Chicken

Teriyaki is a Seattle specialty. The dish is said to have origins in Japan and Hawaii. In fact, the word "teriyaki" refers to a Japanese cooking method, and can be loosely translated as "glazing" and then "grilling." American teriyaki sauce is sweeter and often made with pineapple juice. Since the opening of Toshi's Teriyaki Restaurant in Seattle in 1976, hundreds of restaurants have followed in its footsteps, serving their own versions of teriyaki chicken, pork, or beef.

Serves 4

Ingredients

¾ cup soy sauce

¼ cup pineapple juice

¾ cup sugar

4 cloves garlic, minced

1 tablespoon grated fresh ginger

¼ teaspoon black pepper

1 (3-inch) cinnamon stick

1 cup water, divided

8 boneless, skinless chicken thighs

2 tablespoons cornstarch

Did You Know? In Seattle it's not unusual to find teriyaki garnished with black or white sesame seeds and some sliced scallions.

Preparation

1 In a small saucepan over high heat, combine soy sauce, pineapple juice, sugar, garlic, ginger, pepper, and cinnamon. Bring to a boil, reduce heat to low, and simmer 3 minutes or until sugar is dissolved, stirring occasionally. Remove from heat and let cool. Discard cinnamon stick and mix in ½ cup water.

2 Place chicken in a large resealable plastic bag. Add soy sauce mixture, seal bag, and toss to coat evenly. Refrigerate 4 hours or overnight.

3 Remove chicken to a plate and set aside. Pour soy sauce mixture into a small saucepan and, over medium-high heat, bring to a boil, then reduce heat to low. In a small bowl, mix cornstarch with remaining ½ cup water and add mixture to saucepan. Stir until mixture begins to thicken. Remove from heat and set a ½ cup of the sauce aside for drizzling when ready to serve.

4 Heat a grill pan or skillet over medium heat. Brush chicken with remaining sauce that wasn't set aside, and cook 4 to 5 minutes per side or until no longer pink in center. Slice chicken into strips, drizzle with reserved sauce, and serve.

Country Captain Chicken

Many people think that Country Captain Chicken originated in the Deep South, but, truth is, this curried chicken stew actually came from India. How it got to the South is a bit of a mystery, but most folks agree that it was brought by a sea captain who arrived at either the Charleston or Savannah ports. Since its arrival in the U.S., it's gone through some changes, including the addition of raisins, almonds, and tomatoes. Get ready for lots of flavor!

Serves 6

Ingredients

3 boneless, skinless chicken breasts

¼ cup all-purpose flour

1 teaspoon salt

¼ teaspoon black pepper

4 tablespoons butter, divided

1 green bell pepper, chopped

½ cup chopped onion

2 cloves garlic, minced

2-½ teaspoons curry powder

½ teaspoon dried thyme leaf

1 (28-ounce) can diced tomatoes

½ cup raisins

6 cups hot cooked basmati rice

Preparation

1 Cut chicken into ½-inch strips diagonally.

2 In a large bowl, combine flour, salt, and pepper; mix well. Add chicken and toss until evenly coated. In a large skillet over medium-high heat, melt 2 tablespoons butter; cook chicken 5 to 6 minutes or until browned, but not cooked through. Remove to a plate and set aside.

3 Lower the heat to medium-low and melt remaining 2 tablespoons butter. Add bell pepper, onion, garlic, curry powder, and thyme; cook 5 minutes, stirring occasionally. Add tomatoes, raisins, and the browned chicken, and cook 10 minutes or until the chicken is no longer pink in center, stirring occasionally. Serve over rice.

Serving Suggestion: *To serve this like they do in the South, sprinkle on some slivered almonds before serving. They add a nice crunch!*

Sheet Pan
Greek Dinner

The coastal town of Tarpon Springs, Florida is known for its thriving Greek community. Greek divers were brought to the town in the late 19th century to help harvest sea sponges. Today, there are more Greek Americans living here than anywhere else in the country. And because of that, there's no shortage of great Greek food or fun in Tarpon Springs. This all-in-one, one-pan dinner is inspired by some of our favorite Greek flavors - opa!

Serves 4

Ingredients

½ cup olive oil

3 tablespoons fresh lemon juice

2 teaspoons dried oregano

1 teaspoon dried basil

2 teaspoons salt

½ teaspoon black pepper

4 bone-in chicken breasts
(3-½- to 4-pounds)

1-½ pounds creamer potatoes, cut in half

12 ounces fresh green beans, trimmed

½ red onion, cut into chunks

Preparation

1 Preheat oven to 400 degrees F. Coat a rimmed baking sheet with cooking spray.

2 In a large bowl, combine oil, lemon juice, oregano, basil, salt, and pepper; mix well and reserve 2 tablespoons mixture. Add chicken to bowl and mix until evenly coated. Place on baking sheet, skin-side up. Add potatoes to bowl and toss until evenly coated, then arrange potatoes around chicken on baking sheet. Roast 40 minutes.

3 Meanwhile, in a medium bowl, toss green beans and onion in reserved 2 tablespoons oil mixture. Remove baking sheet from oven, turn potatoes over, and then add green bean mixture to baking sheet. Roast 20 to 25 more minutes or until chicken is no longer pink in center. Bring the pan right out to the table and serve. (Don't forget a trivet!).

Test Kitchen Tip: *If you want to use fresh herbs rather than dried ones, you'll need to use 2 tablespoons of fresh oregano and 1 tablespoon slivered basil. Also, to give this even more lemony goodness, slice up a lemon and roast that along with everything else.*

California Cobb Salad

This salad was created in a giant, hat-shaped restaurant. No, really! Robert H. Cobb invented this salad at the Brown Derby restaurant in 1937. After a particularly long day with nothing to eat, Cobb decided to make himself a salad using the leftovers in the refrigerator. Instead of keeping this one "under his hat," he shared his creation with Sid Grauman (the guy behind Grauman's Chinese Theatre in Hollywood!) who loved it so much, Cobb decided to add it to his menu.

Serves 6

Ingredients

2 boneless, skinless chicken breasts, lightly pounded

Salt and pepper for sprinkling

1 head Romaine lettuce, cut into bite-sized pieces

6 slices crispy cooked bacon, crumbled

3 hard-boiled eggs, coarsely chopped

1 avocado, peeled, pitted, and cut into chunks

2 large tomatoes, cut into chunks

¼ pound blue cheese, crumbled

½ cup red wine vinaigrette

Preparation

1 Season chicken with salt and pepper. Coat a large skillet with cooking spray; cook chicken over medium-high heat 3 to 4 minutes per side or until golden and no pink remains. Remove chicken, set aside to cool slightly, then cut into ½-inch chunks.

2 Meanwhile, arrange lettuce on a large serving platter. Place cooked chicken across center of lettuce. Place bacon, eggs, avocado, tomato, and blue cheese in rows on both sides of chicken.

3 When ready to serve, drizzle with vinaigrette.

So Many Options: Although a red wine vinaigrette is traditional, it's ok to shake things up by serving this with a selection of dressings. What's your favorite?

No visit to Oklahoma City would be complete without a hearty helpin' of chicken fried steak. Here, Howard helps Marie, from Ann's Chicken Fry House, deliver an order of this Route 66 favorite!

Before we moo-ved on to our next stop in Vermont, Howard had some fun sticking his head into this cow cut-out. It was udderly hilarious!

We discovered that if you speak the universal language of food, any cook will welcome you into their kitchen.

It's a good thing we brought our appetites and our cameras to Chicago! There were so many great sights to take in. Check out our Chicago deep-dish pizza on page 182.

We stopped in Intercourse, PA to check out this smoked meats and cheese shop. Everyone left with a full belly!

Mouthwatering Meat

Yankee-Style Pot Roast

In New England this is considered an essential winter meal. And since it's so hearty and comforting, we can't really argue with that. A Yankee pot roast is about more than just the meat. This pot roast features root veggies (often whatever is on hand) that are cooked alongside the beef. The process is slow, but ultimately rewarding. Cook up this one-pot meal whenever you've got a craving for old-fashioned goodness that really satisfies.

Serves 6

Ingredients

1 (3- to 4-pound) beef chuck roast

Salt and pepper for sprinkling

4 tablespoons vegetable oil, divided

1 cup chopped onion

4 cloves garlic, minced

2 teaspoons chopped fresh rosemary

2 teaspoons chopped fresh thyme

1 cup red wine

4 cups beef broth

2 tablespoons tomato paste

3 carrots, cut into 2-inch pieces

2 celery stalks, cut into 2-inch pieces

1-½ cups pearl onions, fresh or frozen

1 bay leaf

Preparation

1 Preheat oven to 350 degrees F.

2 Sprinkle beef with salt and pepper on both sides. In a Dutch oven over medium-high heat, heat 2 tablespoons oil until hot. Add beef and brown on both sides. Remove to a plate.

3 Reduce heat to medium, add remaining 2 tablespoons oil, and cook chopped onion, garlic, rosemary, and thyme 5 minutes, stirring occasionally. Add wine to mixture and stir, making sure to scrape any brown bits from bottom of pan. Stir in broth and tomato paste; return beef to pot.

4 Cover and place in oven. Roast 1-½ hours. Remove pot from oven; add carrots, celery, pearl onions, and bay leaf. Cover and return to oven; cook 1 more hour or until beef and vegetables are fork-tender. Discard bay leaf and slice beef across the grain. Serve with vegetables and gravy from pot.

Big Island Loco Moco

Hawaii's most popular comfort food is an East-meets-West mash-up that's crazy-delicious. It was originally created for teenagers who needed something budget-friendly and filling. In fact, the dish is named after the first boy who ate it; his nickname was "Loco"(the "Moco" was added on because folks liked the way it rhymed!). Today, you'll see everyone from surfers to business professionals going to town on this hearty smothered burger.

Serves 4

Ingredients

1 pound ground beef

½ teaspoon garlic powder

½ teaspoon onion powder

½ teaspoon salt

¼ teaspoon black pepper

2 cups cooked rice, warmed

2 tablespoons butter

4 eggs

1 cup beef gravy, warmed

Preparation

1 In a medium bowl, combine ground beef, garlic powder, onion powder, salt, and pepper; mix well, but don't overmix. Form mixture into 4 hamburger patties.

2 In a large skillet over medium heat, cook patties 8 to 10 minutes or to desired doneness, turning once during cooking.

3 Evenly divide rice on 4 plates, then top with patties; cover to keep warm.

4 Wipe skillet clean, then melt butter over medium heat. Cook eggs in batches, sunny side up, 2 to 3 minutes or until desired doneness. Place eggs over hamburger patties and top with gravy. Serve immediately.

So Many Options: *You can make the rice however you want – in a rice cooker or on the stove. You can even start with a precooked rice package if you want to make things even easier. Then, all you have to do is heat and serve.*

Slow-Roasted Texas Brisket

There are a few things you should know about Texas-style brisket. First, it's always beef. Second, it's always cooked with a dry rub, and not smothered in sauce. Third, it's always cooked low and slow (usually in a smoker, but the oven works great too!). Brisket is no joking matter in the Lone Star State and folks are known to wait in long lines for really tasty brisket. Luckily, you won't have to!

Serves 10

Ingredients

- 2 tablespoons chili powder
- 1 tablespoon garlic powder
- 1 tablespoon onion powder
- 1 tablespoon sugar
- 2 teaspoons dry mustard
- 1 teaspoon smoked paprika
- 1 tablespoon salt
- 2 teaspoons black pepper
- 1 (4- to 5-pound) beef brisket, trimmed
- ½ cup water

Preparation

1 Preheat oven to 325 degrees F.

2 In a small bowl, combine chili powder, garlic powder, onion powder, sugar, dry mustard, paprika, salt, and pepper; mix well.

3 Rub seasoning mixture on both sides of brisket and wrap it tightly in heavy duty aluminum foil. Place in roasting pan and add water to pan.

4 Roast 4 hours or until fork-tender. Carefully unwrap meat (the steam will be very hot) and allow to rest 5 minutes before carving it across the grain.

Serving Suggestion: In Texas, brisket is traditionally served on a tray lined with butcher paper, alongside pickles, white bread, or other popular barbecue sides. You can enjoy this as-is, pile it on a crusty roll, or serve it open-faced on some Texas toast.

Three-Way Cincinnati Chili

Cincinnati, Ohio is considered by many to be the "Chili Capital of the World." The city is said to be home to more than 150 chili establishments. What sets Cincinnati chili apart from some of the other guys is its unique blend of spices and its saucy consistency. (Oh yeah, and the toppings!) In this recipe we serve ours over spaghetti (which is traditional!), but many people enjoy it spooned over hot dogs, burgers, or even toast!

Serves 6

Ingredients

2 cups water

2 pounds ground beef

1 cup chopped onion

1 (28-ounce) can crushed tomatoes

2 tablespoons apple cider vinegar

1 tablespoon Worcestershire sauce

¼ cup chili powder

1 tablespoon unsweetened cocoa powder

1 teaspoon ground cumin

1 teaspoon ground cinnamon

¼ teaspoon ground cloves

1-½ teaspoons salt

½ teaspoon cayenne pepper

1 pound spaghetti

½ cup shredded cheddar cheese

Preparation

1 In a soup pot over medium-high heat, bring water, ground beef, and onion to a boil; cook 30 minutes or until meat is broken up into small pieces, stirring occasionally.

2 Add crushed tomatoes, vinegar, Worcestershire sauce, chili powder, cocoa powder (yes, cocoa powder), cumin, cinnamon, cloves, salt, and cayenne pepper; mix well, and bring to a boil. Reduce heat to low and simmer 1-½ hours, stirring occasionally.

3 Meanwhile, cook spaghetti according to package directions. Serve chili over hot spaghetti and sprinkle with cheese.

Did You Know? *Most authentic Cincinnati chili restaurants will have you order by number. A "Two-Way Chili" consists of chili and spaghetti, a "Three-Way Chili" adds cheddar cheese, a "Four-Way Chili" adds chopped onions, and a "Five-Way Chili" adds beans.*

Oklahoma's Chicken-Fried Steak

Many states have an official state food, and some even have an official state dessert or snack, but Oklahoma takes it one step further by having an official state meal. And one of the foods included on the menu is chicken-fried steak. Although its origins don't necessarily trace back to the state, Oklahomans are big fans of this classic comfort food. You'll find this dish being served at restaurants all over the state.

Serves 4

Ingredients

2 cups buttermilk

2 eggs

2 teaspoons hot sauce

4 (4-ounce) cubed steaks, pounded lightly

1 cup all-purpose flour

1 teaspoon garlic powder

1-½ teaspoons salt

½ teaspoon cayenne pepper

½ teaspoon black pepper

1 cup vegetable oil

COUNTRY GRAVY
¼ cup finely chopped onion

3 tablespoons all-purpose flour

1 cup chicken broth

1 cup milk

¼ teaspoon salt

¼ teaspoon black pepper

Preparation

1 In a large bowl, whisk buttermilk, eggs, and hot sauce. Add steaks to mixture, making sure they're completely covered. Refrigerate 15 minutes.

2 Meanwhile, in a shallow dish, combine 1 cup flour, the garlic powder, 1-½ teaspoons salt, cayenne pepper, and the ½ teaspoon black pepper; mix well.

3 Preheat oven to 250 degrees F.

4 In a cast iron or heavy deep skillet, heat oil until hot, but not smoking. Remove steaks from buttermilk mixture, coat with flour mixture, dip again in buttermilk mixture, then back into flour mixture. Sauté steaks 3 to 4 minutes per side or until cooked through and golden. Drain on paper towels, then place on baking sheet. Place in oven to keep warm.

5 To make the Country Gravy, drain off all but ¼ cup oil from skillet. Add onion and cook over medium heat 3 minutes or until tender. Stir in flour and cook 1 minute. Stir in chicken broth, milk, ¼ teaspoon salt, and ¼ teaspoon black pepper; bring to a boil. Reduce heat to low and simmer 2 to 3 minutes or until thickened. Spoon gravy over steaks.

The American Family Meatloaf

Meatloaf has been in the U.S. since the 1800s, after the invention of the meat grinder. Since then it's gone through a lot. It's been made using pantry staples and dressed up with exotic ingredients. It's been served in casual diners and offered on the menu of gourmet restaurants. It's provided comfort during the Depression and through many of life's rough times. For many Americans, meatloaf is wonderful because of its versatility and its ability to make us feel at home.

Serves 6

Ingredients

1 pound ground beef

1 pound ground pork

½ cup chopped onion

1 slice bread, finely crumbled

1 egg

¼ cup milk

½ cup ketchup, divided

1 teaspoon Worcestershire sauce

½ teaspoon salt

½ teaspoon black pepper

1 tablespoon light brown sugar

2 strips bacon

Preparation

1 Preheat oven to 350 degrees F. Coat a 9- x 5-inch loaf pan with cooking spray.

2 In a large bowl, combine the beef, pork, onion, bread crumbs, egg, milk, ¼ cup ketchup, the Worcestershire sauce, salt, and pepper; gently mix well. Press mixture into pan.

3 In a small bowl, combine remaining ¼ cup ketchup and the brown sugar; spoon over meatloaf. Top with bacon strips.

4 Bake 60 to 65 minutes or until juices run clear. Allow to sit 5 minutes, remove from pan, then slice and serve.

San Antonio's Chili Con Carne

You won't find any beans in this chili! Instead, you'll find lots of beef, spices, and peppers - oh, and a little hot sauce to give it some zing. San Antonio was first introduced to chili by "Chili Queens," women who would feed soldiers at the Military Plaza in the 1800s. Their chili stands were popular for several decades, and inspired the creation of chili establishments in Texas. Chili has become such a Texas tradition that it was officially recognized as the state dish in 1977.

Serves 6

Ingredients

¼ cup vegetable oil

3 pounds lean beef chuck roast, well trimmed and cut into 1-inch cubes

1 onion, chopped

3 cloves garlic, minced

3 tablespoons chili powder

2 teaspoons ground cumin

2 teaspoons salt

2 teaspoons hot pepper sauce

2 cups beef broth

2 cups water

1 (4-ounce) can chopped green chilies, undrained

Preparation

1 In a soup pot over medium-high heat, heat oil until hot; add beef and cook 5 minutes. Drain off liquid; add onion and garlic and sauté 5 minutes or until beef is browned on all sides and onion is tender, stirring frequently.

2 Stir in chili powder, cumin, salt, and hot sauce; cook 1 minute. Add beef broth, water, and chilies with their liquid, and bring to a boil, stirring occasionally. Reduce heat to low, cover, and simmer 45 minutes, then remove cover and simmer an additional 45 minutes or until beef is fork-tender.

Did You Know? *True Texas-style chili is best when you start by roasting fresh peppers, but we took a shortcut by using canned chilies and hot pepper sauce.*

Juicy Lucy Cheeseburgers

There's nothing like a juicy burger patty smothered in melty cheese, except for maybe a juicy burger patty that's stuffed with melty cheese! Meet the Juicy Lucy, a Minneapolis creation that's been around for close to a century. One bite into this bad boy and you'll understand what all the fuss is about. Just be sure to let it cool a bit before opening wide, since the cheese center can be pretty hot when it's taken right off the pan.

Serves 4

Ingredients

1-½ pounds ground beef

1 tablespoon Worcestershire sauce

1 teaspoon garlic powder

½ teaspoon salt

½ teaspoon black pepper

4 slices American cheese

4 hamburger buns, split

Preparation

1 In a large bowl, combine beef, Worcestershire sauce, garlic powder, salt, and pepper; mix well. Form into 8 thin patties.

2 Cut each slice of cheese into 4 equal pieces; make 4 stacks with the pieces. Place one stack of cheese on the center of each of 4 patties. Top the patties with the cheese on them with another patty and tightly pinch the edges together to seal cheese between the burgers.

3 In a large skillet over medium heat, cook burgers 4 to 5 minutes or until they get crispy and well browned. Turn burgers and cook 3 to 4 more minutes or until desired doneness. Place burgers on buns and serve immediately.

Serving Suggestion: Make these burgers deluxe by piling on some sliced tomato and lettuce or any of your favorite burger toppings.

Nebraska Runza Sandwiches

These sandwiches have some Old World roots. Runzas, which are also known as bierocks, were introduced to the Midwest by German-Russian immigrants. In the beginning, they were especially popular with field workers who would take them for lunch. These days, everyone loves them! After all, how can you go wrong with a bread pocket that's loaded with a mouthwatering mixture of beef, onions, and cabbage?

Serves 4

Ingredients

½ pound ground beef

½ cup chopped onion

2 cups chopped cabbage

½ teaspoon garlic powder

¾ teaspoon salt

½ teaspoon black pepper

1 (13.8-ounce) can refrigerated classic pizza crust

Vegetable oil for brushing

Preparation

1 Preheat oven to 400 degrees F. Coat a baking sheet with cooking spray.

2 In a large skillet over medium heat, cook beef and onion 5 minutes, stirring occasionally. Add cabbage, garlic powder, salt, and pepper; cook an additional 10 minutes or until meat is browned and cabbage is tender, stirring occasionally.

3 Unroll dough onto a cutting board and slightly stretch to 8- x 16-inches. Cut into 4 (4- x 8-inch) pieces. Divide meat mixture equally down the center of each piece of dough. Fold 1 long side of the dough over the meat mixture, then fold in the 2 ends and roll up tightly, pinching the seams together. Place seam side down on baking sheet. Lightly brush with oil.

4 Bake 13 to 15 minutes or until golden brown.

Serving Suggestion: Set out your favorite condiments for dipping. We like ours with spicy mustard.

Minnesota Hotdish

What's the most comforting meal you can eat in Minnesota? The answer is a hotdish, and folks have been dishing it up for as long as they can remember (though the name "hotdish" wasn't really used until the 1930s). It's a one-dish meal that traditionally combines some form of meat, a can of creamed soup, mixed veggies, and a starch. This isn't the kind of dish you make a fuss about - it's the kind you throw together for dinner, the church potluck, or a family reunion.

Serves 6

Ingredients

1-½ pounds ground beef

1 teaspoon onion powder

¼ teaspoon salt

¼ teaspoon black pepper

2 (10-¾-ounce) cans cream of mushroom soup

½ cup milk

1 (16-ounce) package frozen mixed vegetables

1 cup (4-ounces) shredded cheddar cheese

½ (32-ounce) package frozen seasoned potato tots

Preparation

1 Preheat oven to 400 degrees F. Coat a 9- x 13-inch baking dish with cooking spray.

2 In a large skillet over medium heat, brown ground beef with onion powder, salt, and pepper, stirring until meat crumbles and is no longer pink; drain. Spoon into baking dish.

3 In a medium bowl, combine soup and milk; mix well. Top the ground beef with the frozen vegetables, pour the soup mixture over that and sprinkle on the cheese. Place the potato tots on top.

4 Bake 40 to 45 minutes or until potato tots are golden and hotdish is heated through.

So Many Options: No two hot dishes have to be alike! It's common for folks to use whatever is in the fridge or on sale at the market, so don't be afraid to change things up. Maybe you can start with different veggies or another variety of cream soup?

Hot Diggity Hot Dogs!

Who would've thought that there could be so many different ways to serve a hot dog? In cities and ballparks all over the country, folks are enjoying their favorite versions, whether that means they stick to the basics or load up their dogs with lots of toppings. From the toppings to the dog itself, everyone's got an opinion, and there's no one right or wrong way to go about it. Here are just some of the popular varieties you'll find in the U.S.

Atlanta Hot Dogs

To enjoy a hot dog like you might find at the ballpark, place a steamed hot dog in a hot dog bun, give it a squirt of yellow mustard, and pile on the coleslaw. It may sound simple, but the combo is always a grand slam.

New York Hot Dogs

Want the true taste of New York? Place a steamed hot dog in a hot dog bun, top it with some spicy brown mustard and a generous amount of what New Yorkers call Pushcart Onion Sauce, which is lots of sautéed onions with a little ketchup and lots of spices. Boy, is it good!

Kansas City Hot Dogs

The ultimate Kansas City hot dog is first grilled and served in a sesame hot dog bun. Then, it's topped with shredded Swiss cheese, sauerkraut, and a healthy amount of Thousand Island dressing. You better open wide for this one!

Chicago Hot Dogs

Only in the Windy City will you find a dog like this. It starts off with a steamed hot dog that's placed in a poppy seed bun. Then, it gets a squirt of yellow mustard, a good amount of bright green relish, and some chopped onions. If you think they stop there, you're nuts. They go on to add a couple of tomato wedges, a pickle spear, and a couple of pickled sports peppers before sprinkling on some celery salt. It's a meal in itself.

Detroit Hot Dogs

Not only do they know how to build cars in Detroit, but they also know how to build a tasty dog. There, they begin by either steaming or grilling their dogs (depending on who you ask) and placing it in a basic hot dog bun. But the bun is the only thing that's basic about this one, since, after it's placed in the bun, it's topped with all-beef chili, chopped red onions, and lots of cheddar cheese.

South Dakota Lamb Chislic

Chislic is unique to South Dakota. Where it came from and how it grew to become a tradition is a bit of a mystery. It's sold in diners, bars, and at fairs all over the state, but especially in the Sioux Falls area. The fried meat cubes are traditionally made with lamb or mutton, but some places are known to use beef (this has caused some debate!). Whether or not you're from South Dakota, we know you'll enjoy this tasty dish!

Serves 4

Ingredients

2 teaspoons Worcestershire sauce

3 cloves garlic, minced

1 teaspoon chili powder

½ teaspoon onion powder

½ teaspoon salt

¼ teaspoon black pepper

1 pound boneless leg of lamb or shoulder, cut into 1-½-inch chunks

2 cups vegetable oil

Preparation

1 In a large bowl, combine Worcestershire sauce, garlic, chili powder, onion powder, salt, and pepper; mix well. Add lamb and toss until evenly coated. Cover and refrigerate 2 hours.

2 In a deep skillet over medium-high heat, heat oil until hot, but not smoking. Cook lamb 2 to 3 minutes until crispy and brown for medium, or until desired doneness, turning once. Drain on a paper towel-lined plate. Serve immediately.

Serving Suggestion: *To serve this in true South Dakota style, make sure you put out some saltines, a bottle of hot sauce, and a shaker filled with garlic salt.*

Nonna's Sunday Gravy

If you grew up in or near any one of the many Italian-American neighborhoods of this country, you might know a thing or two about Sunday Gravy (or Sunday Sauce, depending on where you're from). You might even remember seeing Nonna, standing over a pot, stirring and sneaking a taste every now and then. Her version of Sunday Gravy took half a day to make, but we've come up with one that saves a little time and tastes just as special.

Serves 8

Ingredients

- 6 tablespoons olive oil, divided
- 1 pound pork shoulder steak, cut in half
- 2 teaspoons salt, divided
- ¾ teaspoon black pepper, divided
- 1 pound Italian rope sausage, cut into 6-inch pieces
- 1-½ cups chopped onion
- 8 cloves garlic, minced
- ¾ cup red wine
- 1 (28-ounce) can whole peeled tomatoes
- 1 (28-ounce) can crushed tomatoes
- 1 (28-ounce) can tomato sauce
- 1-½ teaspoons Italian seasoning
- 4 fresh basil leaves, coarsely chopped

Preparation

1. In a large pot over medium-high heat, heat 1 tablespoon oil until hot. Sprinkle pork on both sides with ½ teaspoon salt and ¼ teaspoon pepper. Cook 6 to 8 minutes or until browned, turning once. Remove pork to a plate.

2. Add 1 tablespoon oil to pot and heat until hot. Add sausage and cook 6 to 8 minutes or until browned. Remove sausage to the plate with the pork.

3. In the same pot, over medium-high heat, heat remaining 4 tablespoons oil until hot; add onion and garlic and cook 5 to 7 minutes or until tender. Add wine and cook 2 minutes, scraping the bottom of the pan to loosen all the flavorful bits.

4. Add whole tomatoes, crushed tomatoes, tomato sauce, Italian seasoning, remaining 1-½ teaspoons salt, remaining ½ teaspoon pepper, along with the pork and sausage. Bring to a boil, cover, reduce heat to low, and simmer 2 hours, stirring occasionally. Stir in basil, and cook 30 more minutes, uncovered.

*Serving Suggestion: To add **Homemade Meatballs** to the sauce, gently mix together 1-½ pounds ground beef, ¾ cup bread crumbs, ½ cup Parmesan cheese, ½ cup water, 2 tablespoons chopped parsley, an egg, 2 teaspoons garlic powder, 1 teaspoon salt, and ¾ teaspoons pepper in a large bowl. Gently form into 12 meatballs and bake on a rimmed baking sheet at 350 degrees F for 25 minutes. Add cooked meatballs and pan drippings to the sauce and simmer along with everything else.*

Slow-Cooked Pulled Pork

Pulled pork is a Southern tradition and a dream come true. It's slow cooked for hours until the meat is fall-apart tender, and then it's typically eaten as-is or piled onto a soft bun with coleslaw. No one Southern state can lay claim to this dish, but there are many who argue that the Carolinas have perfected this barbecue favorite. We won't take any sides, but we hope you consider this recipe your invitation to "pig out."

Serves 8

Ingredients

- ¼ cup brown sugar
- 1 tablespoon paprika
- 1 tablespoon chili powder
- 1-½ teaspoons garlic powder
- 1-½ teaspoons salt
- 1 teaspoon black pepper
- 1 (4- to 5-pound) boneless pork butt roast
- 2 onions, thinly sliced
- ¾ cup water
- 2 cups barbecue sauce

Preparation

1. In a small bowl, combine brown sugar, paprika, chili powder, garlic powder, salt, and pepper; mix well. Rub spice mixture over entire roast. Place in a 5-quart or larger slow cooker and top with onions and water.

2. Cover and cook on HIGH 6 hours or until fall-apart tender. Remove pork to a cutting board and shred with 2 forks.

3. Drain liquid from slow cooker, saving onions. Place pork and onions back in slow cooker and add barbecue sauce; mix well. Heat 15 minutes or until warmed through.

Test Kitchen Tip: *If you want to throw this together before work and let it cook all day, go ahead. It can be cooked on LOW 10 to 12 hours, and will be ready just in time to put dinner on the table.*

Depression-Era City Chicken

During the Great Depression, Americans learned how to make do with what they had. Unless you lived in rural areas, chickens were hard to come by. In the cities, butcher shops were more likely to have pork and veal than chicken. This is where American ingenuity came in and City Chicken was born. Pork and veal cubes were breaded and skewered to resemble chicken drumsticks. This "mock chicken" became popular in cities like Pittsburgh, where folks are still enjoying it today.

Serves 6

Ingredients

1 pound boneless pork tenderloin, cut into 1-inch cubes

1 pound veal shoulder, cut into 1-inch cubes

Salt and pepper for sprinkling

½ cup all-purpose flour

1 teaspoon poultry seasoning

2 eggs

1 tablespoon water

1 cup Italian bread crumbs

3 cups vegetable oil

18 skewers (if using wooden ones, soak 15 minutes before using)

Serving Suggestion: These go great with our Honey Mustard Dipping Sauce. It's simply a mixture of ½ cup mayonnaise, 1 tablespoon yellow mustard, and 1 tablespoon honey. Mix it up and it's done.

Preparation

1 Thread 3 cubes of meat onto each skewer, alternating between pork and veal, and place on baking sheet. Lightly sprinkle with salt and pepper on both sides.

2 In a shallow dish, combine flour and poultry seasoning; mix well. In another shallow dish, beat eggs and water. Place bread crumbs in a third shallow dish.

3 Preheat oven to 350 degrees F. In a large deep skillet over medium heat, heat oil until hot, but not smoking (about 350 degrees F).

4 Roll each meat skewer in flour mixture, then egg, then bread crumbs, coating evenly on all sides. Carefully place skewers in oil, in batches, and fry 1 to 2 minutes or until golden brown on both sides. Remove to a baking sheet.

5 Bake 15 to 20 minutes or until meat is no longer pink in center. Serve hot.

Memphis-Style Pork Ribs

The secret to spectacular Memphis-style barbecue is in the rub. While everyone's got their own super-secret blend of spices (good luck trying to get a true pitmaster to reveal theirs!), it's commonly agreed that a good rub should be a little sweet, a little savory, and a little spicy. For folks who prefer their ribs "dry," the rub is enough, but those who like theirs "wet" will happily slather on some barbecue sauce. Either way, you'll love these fall-apart-tender ribs

Serves 4

Ingredients

2 tablespoons smoked paprika

1 tablespoon light brown sugar

2 teaspoons ground cumin

1-½ teaspoons celery salt

1-½ teaspoons garlic powder

1 teaspoon dry mustard

1 tablespoon salt

1-½ teaspoons black pepper

½ teaspoon cayenne pepper

2 racks pork spare ribs (6 to 7 pounds), each rack cut in half

2-½ cups Memphis-style barbecue sauce (see Tip)

Preparation

1 Preheat oven to 325 degrees F.

2 In a small bowl, combine paprika, brown sugar, cumin, celery salt, garlic powder, dry mustard, salt, black pepper, and cayenne pepper; mix well. Rub mixture over both sides of spare ribs then place on baking sheets. Cover tightly with aluminum foil and bake 2 hours.

3 Remove foil, brush ribs with sauce, and continue cooking 45 to 60 minutes or until meat is very tender, brushing occasionally with the sauce. Right before serving, cut into portions and brush with additional sauce for an extra burst of flavor.

*Test Kitchen Tip: To make your own **Memphis-Style Barbecue Sauce** (also known as "mop sauce"), in a saucepan, combine 2 cups ketchup, ½ cup brown sugar, 1/4 cup cider vinegar, 1/4 teaspoon cayenne pepper, 1 tablespoon onion powder, ½ teaspoon celery seed, 1 teaspoon salt, 1-½ teaspoons garlic powder, 1/2 cup yellow mustard, 1 tablespoon chili powder, 1/2 teaspoon black pepper, and 3 tablespoons Worcestershire sauce. Bring to a low boil and simmer 25 minutes, stirring often. Remove from heat and whisk in 2 tablespoons vegetable oil until blended. Sauce will keep for up to two weeks in the refrigerator.*

Saucy Regional Barbecue Sauces

Barbecue sauces come in many different shades. In fact, you could probably make a BBQ rainbow out of all the varieties that are enjoyed around the country! From the sweet red sauces of Texas to the mustardy yellow ones of South Carolina, there are a whole lot of colorful flavors to be enjoyed at a barbecue. Why not set out a few different options at your next cookout or backyard bash?

Eastern North Carolina BBQ Sauce

In eastern North Carolina it's all about the vinegar. This simple barbecue sauce has a bit of a kick, so it's not for the fainthearted.

Makes about 2 cups

1-½ cups apple cider vinegar	1 tablespoon red pepper flakes
½ cup brown sugar	1 teaspoon cayenne pepper
1 tablespoon hot sauce	2 teaspoons salt

In a medium saucepan over medium heat, combine all ingredients and bring to a boil, stirring occasionally. Remove from heat and use or let cool and refrigerate until ready to use.

Western North Carolina BBQ Sauce

Also called "Lexington-Style BBQ Sauce" this sauce is best known for its use of ketchup in the mix, which makes it redder and sweeter than other barbecue sauces.

Makes 1-¼ cups

1 cup ketchup	⅓ cup lemon juice
1 cup packed light brown sugar	1 teaspoon Worcestershire sauce
¼ cup finely chopped onion	1 teaspoon hot pepper sauce
3 tablespoons butter	

In a medium saucepan over medium heat, combine all ingredients and bring to a boil, stirring occasionally. Reduce heat to low and simmer 25 to 30 minutes or until mixture has thickened.

South Carolina Mustard Sauce

If there's a yellow sauce on the table, then you know you're in South Carolina. Mustard is the main ingredient in their BBQ sauce and it gives it a tangy flavor that puts a smile on everyone's faces.

Makes about 1-¼ cups

¾ cup yellow mustard	¼ cup apple cider vinegar
½ cup honey	2 teaspoons Worcestershire sauce
1 tablespoon light brown sugar	1 teaspoon hot sauce

In a small bowl, combine all ingredients; mix until smooth. Refrigerate until ready to serve.

Alabama White BBQ Sauce

The South loves their mayo, so it should come as no surprise that Alabama has even added it to their BBQ sauce! It's a popular choice on chicken, and is used for everything from marinating to dipping.

Makes 1-½ cups

1-½ cups mayonnaise	1 teaspoon sugar
1 tablespoon spicy brown mustard	1 teaspoon salt
2 teaspoons horseradish, drained	½ teaspoon black pepper
1 clove garlic, minced	¼ cup white vinegar

In a medium bowl, combine all ingredients; whisk until smooth. Refrigerate until ready to use.

Texas-Style BBQ Sauce

There are some parts of Texas where sauce isn't even an option, but in areas like East Texas a sweet and tomato-based BBQ sauce, like our version, is a welcome addition.

Makes about 1-½ cups

1 tablespoon butter	¼ cup lemon juice
1 small onion, chopped	2 tablespoons apple cider vinegar
2 cloves garlic, minced	1 tablespoon yellow mustard
1 jalapeño pepper, seeded and minced	1 tablespoon Worcestershire sauce
1 cup ketchup	2 teaspoons chili powder
¼ cup packed brown sugar	½ teaspoon salt

In a medium saucepan over medium heat, melt butter. Add onion and garlic and cook 3 to 4 minutes or until tender. Stir in remaining ingredients and bring to a boil. Reduce heat to low and simmer, uncovered, 15 to 20 minutes or until slightly thickened.

Sensational Seafood, Pasta, & More

South Carolina's Shrimp and Grits

These days, Southern-style restaurants all over the country offer shrimp and grits on their menu, but that wasn't always the case. It used to be that this dish was pretty unique to the lowcountry areas of South Carolina, where shrimp could often be found in the marshes. As you can imagine, local fishermen loved it, and it became a breakfast staple. With the help of some famous chefs and food writers, shrimp and grits gained popularity and is now enjoyed anytime, anywhere.

Serves 6

Ingredients

1-¼ cups water

1 cup old-fashioned grits

1 teaspoon salt

1-½ cups shredded cheddar cheese

½ stick butter

1 green bell pepper, chopped

½ cup chopped onion

3 cloves garlic, minced

1 (14.5-ounce) can diced tomatoes with chilies

1 pound raw large shrimp, peeled, deveined, and tails removed

Hot sauce (optional)

Preparation

1 In a medium saucepan over medium heat, bring water to a boil; stir in grits and salt, cover, and cook 15 to 18 minutes or until thickened. Remove from heat, add cheese, and stir until melted. Cover to keep warm.

2 Meanwhile, in a large skillet over medium-high heat, melt butter; cook bell pepper, onion, and garlic 5 minutes. Add tomatoes and cook 5 minutes. Add shrimp and cook 4 to 5 minutes or until shrimp turn pink, stirring occasionally. Serve shrimp mixture over grits and drizzle with hot sauce, if desired.

Test Kitchen Tip: When it comes to the shrimp, you can use any size. We prefer to use large because you can really sink your teeth into them!

West Coast Shrimp Louie Salad

This salad is a west coast classic with mysterious origins. It was created in either San Francisco, Portland, or Spokane (that really narrows it down, doesn't it?). We can't blame anyone for wanting to take credit for it, since it's obviously good enough to have stuck around for over a hundred years. The dressing is really something special. It's creamy, sweet, and tangy, which complements the shrimp (sometimes crab!) and greens perfectly.

Serves 2

Ingredients

DRESSING
¼ cup mayonnaise

2 tablespoons chili sauce

1 tablespoon Dijon mustard

1 tablespoon fresh lemon juice

½ teaspoon grated lemon zest

¼ teaspoon salt

⅛ teaspoon black pepper

4 cups mixed baby greens

10 cooked, peeled, and deveined large shrimp

1 avocado, pitted, peeled, and sliced

1 hard-boiled egg, peeled and cut in quarters

1 scallion, finely chopped

Preparation

1 To make the dressing, in a small bowl, whisk mayonnaise, chili sauce, mustard, lemon juice, lemon zest, salt, and pepper; set aside.

2 Arrange mixed greens on 2 plates. Top evenly with shrimp, sliced avocado, hard-boiled egg, and scallion. Drizzle with dressing and serve.

So Many Options: Make this salad your own by adding on some tomatoes, cucumbers or onion slices. You can even swap out the shrimp for crab and make a Crab Louie!

Shortcut Lobster Newburg

Set the right mood for two with a dish that's so fancy, restaurants traditionally serve it out of a chafing dish. Lobster Newburg has a complicated history, one that may or may not involve a wealthy man named Ben Wenberg, a French chef, and a New York restaurant called Delmonico's. Instead of fussing over the details, spend a little extra time in the company of a loved one, enjoying this shortcut version of one of our country's most decadent dinners.

Serves 2

Ingredients

2 slices soft white bread

Cooking spray

1 (15-ounce) can lobster bisque

2 tablespoons heavy cream

2 tablespoons dry sherry

1/8 teaspoon black pepper

1 pound cooked lobster meat, cut into 1-inch chunks

Preparation

1 Preheat oven to 400 degrees F. Lightly coat both sides of bread with cooking spray. Gently press bread into muffin tin cups forming bread cups. Bake 7 to 9 minutes or until golden. Carefully remove bread cups from muffin tin to a plate.

2 Meanwhile, in a saucepan over medium-low heat, combine lobster bisque, cream, sherry, and pepper; cook 5 minutes or until heated through. Stir in lobster chunks and cook 5 more minutes or until heated through. Spoon mixture into bread cups and serve.

***Did You Know?** You can buy cooked lobster at the seafood counter, but if you'd like to cook a fresh lobster, see our easy instructions on page 86.*

Crave-Worthy Creole Catfish

Did you know that most of our farm-raised catfish comes from the Southern states of Alabama, Arkansas, Mississippi, and Louisiana? With catfish being so plentiful in the area, it's no surprise that Southerners have come up with lots of different ways to enjoy it. Here's one that's cooked in the popular Louisiana Creole style. We hope you're ready for a flavor-packed meal!

Serves 4

Ingredients

6 tablespoons butter, softened, divided

1 tablespoon Creole mustard (see note)

2 teaspoons paprika

1 teaspoon dried thyme leaves

½ teaspoon sugar

1 teaspoon salt

½ teaspoon cayenne pepper

½ teaspoon black pepper

4 (6-ounce) U.S. farm-raised catfish fillets

Preparation

1 In a small bowl, combine 4 tablespoons butter and the mustard; mix well. Spoon mixture onto a sheet of plastic wrap and roll into a 3-inch log; seal and refrigerate.

2 In another small bowl, combine paprika, thyme, sugar, salt, cayenne pepper, and black pepper; mix well. In a small microwave-safe bowl, melt remaining 2 tablespoons butter. Brush fish with half the melted butter and sprinkle with half the spice mixture. Pat gently to secure. Turn fish over and repeat.

3 Coat a grill pan with cooking spray and heat over medium-high heat until hot. Cook fish 3 to 4 minutes or until browned. Turn and cook 3 to 4 more minutes, or until fish flakes easily with a fork.

4 Unwrap mustard butter and slice into 4 equal pieces and place a piece on each fillet. Serve immediately.

Did You Know? Creole mustard is a grainy, zesty mustard commonly used in Louisiana. If you don't have any, feel free to use a spicy mustard instead.

Cedar Plank Alaskan Salmon

Fishing is an important part of life for many of the people in Alaska, especially because the seafood industry plays such a large role in the state's economy. While Alaska is known for its wide variety of seafood exports, the species that reigns supreme in the state is the Alaskan King (Chinook) salmon. King salmon are native to the Pacific coast and return to Alaska's freshwater streams to spawn. Their return is famously known as the "salmon run."

Serves 4

Ingredients

4 cedar planks, each about 6- x 8-inches (see Tips)

4 (6-ounce) salmon fillets

½ teaspoon salt

¼ teaspoon black pepper

3 tablespoons butter, melted

1 tablespoon lemon juice

½ teaspoon lemon zest

Preparation

1 In a large container, soak cedar planks in water at least 1 hour or overnight; drain and place on paper towels.

2 Preheat grill to medium. Sprinkle salmon evenly with salt and pepper. Place each piece on a cedar plank.

3 In a small bowl, combine butter, lemon juice, and lemon zest; mix well and brush onto salmon.

4 Place plank on grill rack and cook, covered, 12 to 15 minutes or until fish flakes easily with a fork.

Test Kitchen Tips: *You can get cedar planks at most grocery stores, near the fish counter. If you don't see them, simply ask. When cooking with them, the planks should smoke and char around the edges, but not catch on fire. If they do, spray some water over them with a spray bottle.*

Rosemary & Lemon Trout

The Great Lakes make up the world's largest surface freshwater system in the world, which means it's a great place to go fishing for freshwater fish. One variety of fish that's popular is trout. Trout can be fished all year long in the Great Lakes, and many people travel to states like Michigan to check out the "trout trails." Here's a great way to prepare mild flavored trout that uses fresh rosemary and bright-tasting lemon.

Serves 2

Ingredients

1 tablespoon olive oil

2 (8-ounce) whole trout, butterflied and deboned

Salt and pepper for sprinkling

2 tablespoons butter, melted

1 tablespoon capers

1 clove garlic, minced

1 sprig fresh rosemary, stem removed and leaves finely chopped

1 tablespoon fresh lemon juice

Preparation

1 Preheat oven to 450 degrees F. Brush a rimmed baking sheet with olive oil.

2 Place trout skin-side down on baking sheet and lightly sprinkle with salt and pepper. In a small bowl, combine butter, capers, garlic, and rosemary; mix well. Spoon butter mixture evenly over trout and drizzle with lemon juice.

3 Bake 10 to 12 minutes or until fish flakes easily with a fork. Serve immediately.

Test Kitchen Tip: *If you've caught some fresh trout while camping and don't want to wait to cook it at home, you can cook these over a campfire. Simply sauté them in a cast iron skillet over the glowing embers. Flip the fish once and it's done. (Careful, the pan will be mighty hot!)*

Marinated Ahi Tuna Poke

Poke, which is pronounced "po-kay," means "to cut crosswise into pieces" in the Hawaiian language. It is one of Hawaii's most popular snack foods and it's been around for centuries. Hawaiians consider it to be a comfort food, which is why you'll find it everywhere from special get-togethers to the local convenience store. In recent years, ahi tuna has become the seafood of choice for poke, especially on the mainland. This is so fresh-tasting and flavorful, it's hard not to fall in love!

Serves 6

Ingredients

3 tablespoons soy sauce

2 tablespoons sesame oil

¼ cup chopped sweet onion

2 teaspoons sesame seeds, toasted

1 tablespoon chopped macadamia nuts (optional)

2 cloves garlic, minced

½ teaspoon grated fresh ginger

½ teaspoon kosher salt

1 pound ahi tuna steaks, cut into ½-inch cubes

1 scallion, thinly sliced (optional)

Preparation

1 In a large bowl, combine soy sauce, sesame oil, onion, sesame seeds, macadamia nuts (if desired), garlic, ginger, and salt; mix well. Add tuna and mix until thoroughly combined.

2 Cover and refrigerate at least 2 hours or overnight. Right before serving, sprinkle on scallion (if desired).

Serving Suggestion: *Turn this snack into a meal by serving it with an assortment of fresh veggies— everything from sliced cucumbers and shredded carrot to sliced avocado and pepper strips. Yum!*

Utica's Chicken Riggies

Anyone from upstate New York would easily be able to tell you about "riggies." This rigatoni pasta dish is somewhat of a celebrity in cities like Utica and Rome. In fact, it's been celebrated with its own festival for over 10 years. The dish is traditionally made with chicken and features a spicy marinara sauce. While there are a few different stories about who came up with it, it's generally agreed that it was first introduced sometime in the late 70s.

Serves 6

Ingredients

1 pound rigatoni pasta

3 tablespoons olive oil

1 cup chopped onion

3 cloves garlic, minced

5 hot cherry peppers, cut in quarters

4 boneless, skinless chicken breasts, cut into 1-inch cubes

½ teaspoon salt

½ teaspoon black pepper

¾ cup chicken broth

½ cup white wine

1 cup marinara sauce

3 tablespoons butter

1 cup Parmesan cheese

¼ cup fresh basil, sliced

Preparation

1 Cook pasta according to package directions; drain.

2 Meanwhile, in a large deep skillet over medium heat, heat oil until hot. Cook onion, garlic, and cherry peppers 5 minutes or until tender.

3 Sprinkle chicken with salt and pepper, and add to skillet; cook 6 to 8 minutes or until no longer pink. Add broth and wine and simmer 5 minutes. Stir in marinara sauce and cook 5 minutes. Add butter, Parmesan cheese, and basil, and cook 6 to 8 minutes or until thickened.

4 Add pasta to the skillet, mix well, and heat 5 minutes or until heated through. Serve piping hot.

Classic
Fettuccine Alfredo

This dish got its start in Italy, in the early 1900s, when a chef named Alfredo di Lelio decided to make it for his wife. She had just had their first child and didn't have much of an appetite, so Alfredo came up with a delicious solution. His wife loved it so much, she asked him to add it to his menu. A couple of famous American actors got a taste of it while on their honeymoon, brought the recipe back with them to New York, and the rest is history.

Serves 4

Ingredients

16 ounces fettuccine

1 stick butter

1 clove garlic, minced

2 cups (1 pint) heavy cream

½ teaspoon black pepper

1-¾ cups grated Parmesan cheese

Preparation

1 Cook fettuccine according to package directions; drain well.

2 Meanwhile, in a large skillet over medium-low heat, melt butter. Add garlic and sauté 1 minute. Add heavy cream and pepper; cook 6 to 8 minutes or until hot, but not boiling, stirring constantly. Stir in cheese and cook 6 to 7 minutes or until sauce has thickened.

3 Place fettuccini a large bowl, pour sauce over it, and toss until well coated. Serve immediately.

Serving Suggestion: Top each bowl with some freshly chopped parsley, ground black pepper, and some extra grated parmesan for a restaurant-special look.

Johnny Marzetti Casserole

This casserole has got some history. It was first served by Teresa Marzetti, an Italian woman who immigrated to Ohio in 1896. In that same year, she opened up her first Italian restaurant just down the street from Ohio State University. Among her many menu items, she included a recipe for "Johnny Marzetti," a casserole named after her brother-in-law. For many Ohioans, this beefy and cheesy macaroni casserole is a childhood favorite that's full of comfort.

Serves 8

Ingredients

1 pound elbow macaroni

3 tablespoons olive oil

1 cup chopped onion

¾ pound mushrooms, sliced

2 pounds ground beef

1 (24-ounce) jar spaghetti sauce

1 teaspoon garlic powder

4 cups shredded cheddar cheese, divided

Preparation

1 Cook macaroni according to package directions, drain well.

2 Preheat oven to 375 degrees F. Coat a 9- x 13-inch baking dish with cooking spray. Meanwhile, in a large skillet over medium-high heat, heat oil until hot; cook onion and mushrooms 5 minutes or until tender. Remove to a large bowl and set aside.

3 Add beef to skillet and cook 6 to 8 minutes or until no longer pink, stirring occasionally; drain off excess liquid. Place beef in bowl with vegetables. Add spaghetti sauce, garlic powder, and 3 cups cheese; mix well. Stir in macaroni until thoroughly combined.

4 Spoon mixture into baking dish, cover with aluminum foil, and cook 25 minutes. Remove foil, sprinkle with remaining 1 cup cheese, and continue to cook 25 more minutes or until heated through.

Wisconsin Mac 'n' Cheese

Wisconsin loves its cheese. The state is home to more than 100 cheese factories and over 600 cheese varieties! Many of the state's residents even refer to themselves as "cheeseheads." Inspired by all the cheesy goodness that comes out of Wisconsin, we came up with this extra-cheesy, ooey-gooey, mac 'n' cheese that's sure to become a dinner time favorite at your house.

Serves 6

Ingredients

2 slices white bread

5 tablespoons butter, divided

½ cup finely diced onion

2 tablespoons all-purpose flour

1 teaspoon salt

½ teaspoon black pepper

2-½ cups milk

2 teaspoons yellow mustard

3-½ cups shredded Wisconsin extra sharp cheddar cheese, divided

1 pound elbow macaroni, cooked according to package directions and drained

1 cup shredded mozzarella cheese

Preparation

1 Preheat oven to 375 degrees F. Coat a 2-quart baking dish with cooking spray.

2 In a blender or food processor, pulse bread until coarsely crumbled. In a small skillet over medium heat, melt 1 tablespoon butter, then add bread crumbs and heat 2 minutes or until golden, stirring occasionally; set aside.

3 In a soup pot over medium heat, melt remaining 4 tablespoons butter; add onion and cook 5 minutes or until tender. Stir in flour, salt, and pepper, and cook 2 minutes. Gradually add milk and mustard; bring to a boil and cook until thickened, stirring constantly. Stir in 3 cups cheddar cheese and heat until cheese is melted. Remove from heat.

4 Add pasta, and mix until evenly coated. Stir in mozzarella cheese. Pour into baking dish, then top with remaining ½ cup cheddar cheese. Sprinkle with toasted bread crumbs.

5 Cover with aluminum foil and bake 20 minutes; remove foil and continue baking 15 to 20 minutes or until heated through and top is golden.

Barbecue Chicken Pizza

The first pizza, as we know it today, featured simple ingredients like fresh tomatoes, mozzarella cheese, and basil (you might know this as the classic margherita pizza). It was created way back in the 1800s, which means there's been plenty of time for the world to experiment with different toppings. One American combo that's said to have originated in California, is the barbecue chicken pizza. This gourmet-style pie is worth a second slice (or maybe a third one...).

Makes 8 slices

Ingredients

4 tablespoons olive oil, divided

1 cup cooked chicken chunks

¼ cup barbecue sauce

1 jalapeño pepper, seeded and chopped

1 pound store-bought pizza dough

½ cup shredded mozzarella cheese

¼ cup thinly sliced red onion

1 tomato, cut into thin strips, pulp removed

4 ounces goat cheese, crumbled

2 tablespoons fresh cilantro leaves

Parmesan cheese for sprinkling

Preparation

1 Preheat oven to 450 degrees F. Lightly brush a 12- to 14-inch pizza pan with 1 tablespoon olive oil.

2 In a medium bowl, combine chicken, barbecue sauce, and jalapeno; mix well.

3 Place dough on a lightly floured surface. With a rolling pin, roll out dough to a 12- to 14-inch circle. Place on pizza pan. Lightly brush dough with 2 tablespoons olive oil. Sprinkle mozzarella cheese evenly over dough. Top with onion, tomato, chicken mixture, and goat cheese.

4 Bake 14 to 18 minutes or until crust is crisp and golden. Drizzle evenly with remaining 1 tablespoon olive oil, then sprinkle with cilantro and Parmesan cheese. Cut into 8 slices and serve immediately.

Test Kitchen Tip: For the chicken, you can either cook a chicken breast or, easier yet, cut up the breast from a store-bought rotisserie chicken.

Chicago-Style Deep-Dish Pizza

Chicago-style deep dish pizza is unlike any other style of pizza. It's an upside-down version that features a layer of crust, layers of thick mozzarella cheese, a meaty topping, sauce, and a final thin layer of Parmesan cheese. This pizza is typically a couple of inches thick and is served in slices like any other pie. Ike Sewell and Ric Riccardo, the founders of Pizzeria Uno, are credited with creating the deep-dish pizza in the 1940s. Pizza in Chicago hasn't been the same since.

Makes 8 slices

Ingredients

1 pound hot Italian sausage, casings removed

1 green bell pepper, cut into ¼-inch strips

½ cup chopped onion

1 pound store-bought pizza dough

10 slices mozzarella cheese

¾ cup pizza or spaghetti sauce

2 tablespoons grated Parmesan cheese

Preparation

1 Preheat oven to 450 degrees F. Coat a 12-inch deep-dish pizza pan with cooking spray.

2 In a large skillet over medium heat, cook sausage, pepper, and onion 6 to 8 minutes or until no pink remains in sausage, stirring constantly; drain and set aside.

3 Using your fingertips or the heel of your hand, spread dough so it covers bottom of the pan and comes three-quarters of the way up the sides. (You must line the sides or it won't be deep-dish.) Top the dough with the mozzarella cheese, then spoon the sausage mixture over that. Spoon sauce evenly over sausage and sprinkle with Parmesan cheese.

4 Bake 22 to 25 minutes or until crust is crisp and golden. Cut into 8 slices and serve immediately.

So Many Options: Not crazy about the hot stuff? Use a milder sausage for the same super Chicago taste.

The next time you're thinking of taking a family road trip, pack up the car and head down Route 66. It's as All-American as you can get with lots of tasty stops along the way!

There's nothing better than a freshly-picked tomato, whether it's in Florida or Upstate New York. Just add a little salt and pepper for extra goodness.

We sure picked the right day to hit the streets of Boston. It was picture-perfect! After visiting Quincy Market and Back Bay, we were glad we wore our stretchy pants.

We were surprised to discover some great food options at some of our favorite National Parks. From grilled bison to fresh salmon, everything was amazing! Don't forget to try our salmon on page 166.

Check out Kelly as she makes friends with Hobbs. She's just as comfortable in the stable as she is in the kitchen or behind the camera.

Great Go-Alongs

Boston Baked Beans

Legend has it that Native Americans were making baked beans long before the Pilgrims landed, and that Boston baked beans are an adaptation of the original recipe. What sets Boston's recipes for baked beans apart is their use of molasses. Molasses is a by-product of sugarcane that became a staple in many New Englanders' favorite foods. Bostonians loved their baked beans so much that people began to call the city "Beantown." To the dismay of many locals, the nickname stuck.

Serves 8

Ingredients

2 cups navy beans
(1 pound package)

¾ cup finely diced onion

6 slices bacon, coarsely chopped

1-½ cups ketchup

⅓ cup molasses

2 tablespoons Worcestershire sauce

1 cup brown sugar

1 teaspoon dry mustard

1 teaspoon salt

¼ teaspoon black pepper

1 cup water

Preparation

1 Place beans in a large bowl and add enough water to cover. Soak overnight; drain.

2 In a large saucepan over high heat, add beans and enough water to cover; bring to a boil. Cover, reduce heat to low, and simmer 1 hour; drain.

3 In a 4-quart or larger slow cooker, place beans, onion, and bacon. In a medium bowl, combine remaining ingredients, including the 1 cup water; mix well and pour over beans. Stir until thoroughly combined.

4 Cover and cook on LOW 8 to 9 hours or until beans are soft and mixture is thickened.

Cowboy Corn Fritters

While corn fritters are more commonly associated with the South, we're going to fill you in on another group of people who love these - cowboys. Back in the days of horses and chuck wagons, corn fritters were a must-have. They tasted great, were easy to store, and could keep a hungry cowboy full until the next meal. Cowboy-style corn fritters were pretty basic, so we jazzed ours up a little to make them really tasty.

Makes 2 dozen

Ingredients

1-¾ cups all-purpose flour

2 teaspoons baking powder

1 teaspoon salt

¼ teaspoon black pepper

¼ teaspoon cayenne pepper

2 eggs, beaten

¼ cup salsa

1 (14-¾-ounce) can cream-style corn

1 cup fresh or frozen corn (thawed if frozen)

¼ cup vegetable oil, or more as needed

Preparation

1 In a large bowl, combine flour, baking powder, salt, black pepper, and cayenne pepper. Add eggs and salsa; mix well. Stir in both types of corn.

2 In a large skillet over medium heat, heat 1 tablespoon oil until hot. Drop batter into hot skillet 1 tablespoonful at a time and cook 4 to 5 minutes or until golden, turning fritters halfway through cooking. Remove to a covered platter.

3 Add another tablespoon of oil to skillet. When hot, repeat with remaining batter, adding more oil as needed, until all batter is used.

Serving Suggestion: *Enjoy these as-is or top them with some sour cream and chives for even more goodness.*

Roasted Vidalia Onions

Imagine the surprise on Moses Coleman's face, back in 1931, when he discovered that the onions he had planted were sweet instead of hot. At the time, he probably had no idea that his sweet onion discovery would lead to the production of one of the most popular veggies in the South, the Vidalia® onion. Since Vidalia onions can only be grown in Georgia (20 counties, to be exact!), it's no wonder why it was officially recognized as the state vegetable in 1990.

Makes 3

Ingredients

3 Vidalia onions, unpeeled

1 tablespoon olive oil

½ teaspoon coarse salt

¼ teaspoon black pepper

6 sprigs fresh thyme

Preparation

1 Preheat oven to 375 degrees F.

2 Trim both ends off onions (do not peel), then set each onion on a piece of aluminum foil. Drizzle onions evenly with oil and sprinkle with salt and pepper. Place 2 sprigs of thyme on top of each onion. Wrap each onion loosely in foil and place in baking dish.

3 Bake 70 to 75 minutes, or until a knife can be easily inserted in center of onions. Carefully remove foil from onions and allow to sit until cool enough to touch. Before digging in, remove onion skin and the thyme.

Serving Suggestion: These are just as welcome next to a sizzling steak as they are next to... well, just about anything.

Utica Greens

This is the dish that's going to help you get your family to eat their greens again. In Central New York, you can find it on the menu of practically every Italian restaurant. While the idea for this dish originated with Italian home cooks, many agree that a chef named Joe Morelle made it popular when he added his version to the menu of Chesterfield Restaurant in 1988. Just wait until you taste all of the different flavors in this better-than-ever side dish!

Serves 4

Ingredients

4-¼ cups water, divided

1 head escarole, cut into 1-inch pieces

3 tablespoons olive oil

¼ pound sliced prosciutto, chopped

½ cup chopped onion

3 cloves garlic, minced

5 hot cherry peppers, chopped

¼ teaspoon salt

¼ teaspoon black pepper

1 tablespoon butter

¼ cup bread crumbs

2 tablespoons grated Parmesan cheese

Preparation

1 In a soup pot over high heat, bring 4 cups water to a boil. Add escarole and cook 2 minutes. Drain and rinse with cold water; set aside.

2 In a large skillet over medium heat, heat oil until hot; add prosciutto and onion and cook 5 minutes. Stir in garlic and cook 1 more minute. Add escarole, cherry peppers, the remaining ¼ cup water, the salt, and pepper. Cook 5 minutes or until escarole is tender.

3 Meanwhile, in a small skillet, melt butter. Add bread crumbs and cook 1 to 2 minutes or until lightly toasted, stirring constantly. Sprinkle escarole mixture with bread crumbs and Parmesan cheese, and serve.

Crunchy Fried Okra

Okra is a popular garden vegetable in states like Oklahoma and all over the South. It was brought to America from Africa sometime in the 18th century. Some people know it for its sliminess, which is called mucilage. Southerners discovered that the mucilage was actually great for thickening up dishes like gumbo, burgoo, and Brunswick stew. They also found that frying the okra helped get rid of the slime, and, when battered, it would make the perfect crunchy snack.

Serves 6

Ingredients

1 egg

1 tablespoon milk

½ cup cornmeal

⅓ cup all-purpose flour

¾ teaspoon garlic powder

¾ teaspoon salt

¼ teaspoon black pepper

1 cup vegetable oil

15 fresh okra pods, sliced into ½-inch pieces

Preparation

1 In a small bowl, whisk egg and milk. In a medium bowl, combine cornmeal, flour, garlic powder, salt, and pepper; mix well.

2 In a medium skillet over medium heat, heat oil until hot, but not smoking. Coat okra with egg mixture, then coat evenly with cornmeal mixture. Place in oil and cook 1 minute on each side or until golden. Drain on a paper towel-lined plate.

Serving Suggestion: *We think these are even better when you serve them with some remoulade sauce, and they go great alongside our recipe for Shrimp Po' Boys on page 84. Talk about tasty!*

Good Luck Hoppin' John

If you want good luck in the New Year, Southerners will tell you that you have to eat a bowl of Hoppin' John on the first day of the year. No one is quite sure how this meal of rice, peas, and ham became associated with New Year's, but by the 20th century everyone knew about it. It's also traditional to serve this hearty dish with collard greens and corn bread, which are said to symbolize paper money and gold.

Serves 8

Ingredients

1 tablespoon vegetable oil

1 cup chopped onion

2 celery stalks, chopped

3 cloves garlic, minced

1 cup chopped cooked ham (about ½ pound)

3 (15-ounce) cans black-eyed peas, undrained

1 (15-ounce) can diced tomatoes, undrained

3 cups chicken broth

½ teaspoon crushed red pepper flakes

½ teaspoon salt

¼ teaspoon black pepper

6 cups hot cooked white rice

Preparation

1 In a soup pot over medium-high heat, heat oil until hot; cook onion, celery, and garlic 5 minutes or until tender. Add ham, black-eyed peas, tomatoes, broth, red pepper flakes, salt, and black pepper.

2 Bring to a boil, reduce heat to low, and simmer 25 to 30 minutes. Serve mixture over rice.

Did You Know? *It's generally agreed that the reason this dish is called "Hoppin' John" is due to a mispronunciation of the French-Creole word for pigeon peas, which is "pois à pigeon."*

Iowa's Grilled Corn on the Cob

Iowa grows A LOT of corn. In fact, they've produced more corn than any other state in the country for the last two decades. (We weren't exaggerating!) So you can imagine how important corn must be to the folks that live there. For this recipe, we wanted to keep things simple and show off the great taste of perfectly grilled corn on the cob. Make this for your next cookout or family get-together and you'll have them smiling from ear to ear.

Serves 6

Ingredients

6 ears corn on the cob, not husked (see Tip)

½ stick butter, softened

3 cloves garlic, minced

Sea salt for sprinkling

Coarsely ground black pepper for sprinkling

Preparation

1 In a large pot, place corn in cold water, submerging completely; soak 5 minutes. Preheat grill to medium-high heat. Remove corn from water, shake off excess water. Peel husks back as shown in picture; do not remove them. Place around edges of grill and cover.

2 Grill 10 to 15 minutes or until slightly charred, turning occasionally.

3 Meanwhile, in a small bowl, combine butter and garlic; mix well. Remove corn from heat and carefully remove husks. Brush butter mixture evenly over corn, then sprinkle with salt and pepper. Serve immediately.

Test Kitchen Tip: *We keep the husks on our corn because they serve as handy holders. But don't forget to remove the corn-silks (those are the thread-like fibers), since they can be messy and bothersome.*

Twice-Baked Loaded Potatoes

The potato is one of America's favorite and most widely consumed vegetables. It's not strange for people to have it more than two to three times a week, especially since there are so many different ways to eat it. Potatoes can be served mashed, fried, boiled, baked...you get the idea. The next time you want to show off your potato skills, make these easy, impressive-looking twice-baked potatoes, loaded with all the fixings.

Serves 4

Ingredients

4 large baking potatoes

¼ cup sour cream

3 tablespoons butter

1 teaspoon onion powder

1 teaspoon salt

¼ teaspoon black pepper

1 cup shredded cheddar cheese, divided

5 strips bacon, cooked crispy and crumbled, divided

1 scallion, thinly sliced

Preparation

1 Preheat oven to 400 degrees F. Scrub potatoes then pierce each potato a few times with a fork.

2 Bake 60 to 65 minutes or until tender. Let cool slightly.

3 Cut about ½-inch off top of each potato and scoop out the pulp, leaving a ¼-inch of the pulp so that the shell holds its shape. Place pulp in a medium bowl and add sour cream, butter, onion powder, salt, and pepper, and beat with an electric mixer until smooth. Stir in ¾ cup cheese and ½ the bacon.

4 Spoon mixture evenly into potato shells, leveling it off. Place remaining potato mixture in a pastry bag with a large star tip or in a plastic storage bag with about ¼-inch cut off the corner. Pipe the top of each potato evenly. Sprinkle with remaining cheese and remaining bacon, and bake 20 to 25 minutes or until hot and top is golden. Sprinkle with scallions before serving.

__Did You Know?__ Idaho grows more potatoes than any other state in the country. In fact, it was designated their state vegetable in 2002. The state is even known for hosting a variety of potato-themed events, including a giant potato drop on New Year's Eve.

Utah's Funeral Potatoes

Every bite of this cheesy potato casserole delivers lots of comfort, and that's exactly what the Relief Society of the Mormon Church had in mind when they first started bringing this dish to funerals and wakes. As it turns out, it brought so much comfort that folks started making it for happy occasions too, and it eventually became a Utah staple. The dish was even featured on an Olympic trading pin when Salt Lake City was the host city in 2002.

Serves 8

Ingredients

1 (32-ounce) package frozen diced potatoes, thawed

2 cups shredded sharp cheddar cheese

1 (10-½-ounce) can cream of celery soup

1 (10-½-ounce) can cream of mushroom soup

1 cup sour cream

1 teaspoon onion powder

½ teaspoon salt

¼ teaspoon black pepper

1 stick butter, melted, divided

2 cups cornflakes, coarsely crushed

Preparation

1 Preheat oven to 375 degrees F. Coat a 9- x 13-inch baking dish with cooking spray.

2 In a large bowl, combine potatoes, cheese, both soups, sour cream, onion powder, salt, pepper, and ½ the butter; mix well. Spoon mixture into baking dish.

3 In a medium bowl, combine crushed cornflakes and remaining butter; mix well and sprinkle evenly over potatoes.

4 Cover with aluminum foil and bake 35 minutes. Remove foil and bake 10 to 15 additional minutes or until heated through and the top is golden.

Test Kitchen Tip: *Since these are often taken to a friend's or neighbor's house while hot, it's a good idea to find a baking dish with a carrier or wicker basket holder to transport it. It keeps the dish warm and prevents you from burning yourself while carrying it.*

Old-Fashioned Pierogies

These are inspired by the large Polish communities of cities like Chicago and New York. Pierogies can best be described as Polish dumplings, and are often filled with any combination of cheese, potatoes, onions, cabbage, meat, and more. You can eat them as a snack or have them for dinner; either way, you can't go wrong. When we come across amazing food like this, we feel extra-lucky to live in a country with people from so many different cultures.

Makes about 36

Ingredients

1 stick butter

1-¼ cups finely chopped onion

3 large baking potatoes, peeled and cut into chunks (about 2 pounds)

½ cup shredded cheddar cheese

1-½ teaspoons salt, divided

¼ teaspoon black pepper

3 eggs

1 cup sour cream

3 cups all-purpose flour plus extra for rolling

1 tablespoon baking powder

Preparation

1 In a skillet over medium heat, melt butter and sauté onion 5 to 7 minutes or until tender. Remove ¼ cup of onion and set aside. Continue to cook remaining onion 5 to 7 minutes or until golden; set aside. In a large saucepan, boil potatoes 15 to 20 minutes or until tender; drain and mash.

2 In a large bowl, combine the ¼ cup onion, the mashed potatoes, cheese, 1 teaspoon salt, and the pepper; mix well and set aside.

3 To make the dough, in another large bowl, mix eggs and sour cream until smooth. In a medium bowl, combine 3 cups flour, the baking powder, and remaining ½ teaspoon salt; mix well. Add flour mixture to egg mixture and stir until dough comes together.

4 Place dough on a lightly floured surface and knead until smooth. Divide dough in half and cover half with plastic wrap. Lightly flour your work surface and, with a rolling pin, roll out the dough to 1/8-inch thickness. Using a 3-inch cookie cutter or drinking glass, cut out circles. Place 1 teaspoon potato filling in center of each dough round. Moisten edges with water, fold the dough over the filling and pinch edges together to seal. Repeat with remaining dough and potato mixture.

5 Bring a large pot of salted water to a boil over high heat. Add pierogies in batches and cook 4 minutes. Remove with a slotted spoon to a paper towel-lined platter. Over medium heat, add pierogis to skillet with remaining onion. Cook 3 to 5 minutes or until heated through.

Syracuse Salt Potatoes

No, you can't grow salt potatoes! During the 1800s, salt miners working in the Syracuse salt springs would bring along bags of small potatoes for lunch each day. After boiling their potatoes in the distilling vats, they discovered that doing so made the potatoes creamy on the inside with the perfect salty crust. The idea caught on and these became a Central New York favorite. While they're enjoyed year-round, they're especially popular during the summer at picnics and barbecues.

Serves 6

Ingredients

3 pounds small new potatoes (creamers)

4 quarts water

1-½ cups kosher or sea salt

1 stick butter

Preparation

1 In a large pot over high heat, cover potatoes with water. Pour salt over potatoes and bring to a boil. Cover loosely, reduce heat to medium, and cook 15 to 20 minutes or until potatoes are fork-tender; drain and place on a platter.

2 In the same pot over low heat, melt butter. Drizzle melted butter over the potatoes or serve melted butter in a bowl on the side and dunk away.

Test Kitchen Tip: *For that authentic Central New York flavor you need to use lots of salt. The finished boiled potatoes should have a white salt coating on them. By the way, if you happen to have any of these left over (we doubt it!), you can use them to make home fries.*

Roasted & Glazed Sweet Potato Wedges

Sweet potatoes like it hot, as in, sweet potatoes prefer a hot and moist climate to grow in. That's why more than 50 percent of all sweet potatoes grown in the U.S. come from North Carolina. In the last few decades, sweet potatoes have really grown in popularity too. It used to be that some people only ate them for Thanksgiving, but nowadays you can find some type of sweet potato side dish on almost every menu. One of our favorites is sweet potato wedges!

Serves 4

Ingredients

4 large sweet potatoes (about 2 pounds)

¼ cup vegetable oil

¼ teaspoon black pepper

½ cup maple syrup

2 tablespoons balsamic vinegar

1 tablespoon butter, melted

⅛ teaspoon cayenne pepper

Sea salt for sprinkling

Preparation

1 Preheat oven to 425 degrees F. Coat rimmed baking sheets with cooking spray.

2 Peel potatoes and cut each in half lengthwise. Now cut each half into 4 wedges. In a large bowl, combine potatoes, oil, and black pepper; toss to coat completely. Place potatoes in a single layer onto baking sheets. Do not overcrowd.

3 Bake 30 minutes, gently turn potatoes over, and bake an additional 20 minutes or until tender and crispy.

4 Meanwhile, in a small bowl, combine syrup, vinegar, butter, and cayenne pepper; mix well. Place sweet potato wedges on a serving platter, drizzle with syrup mixture. Sprinkle with salt and serve immediately.

Wild Rice Patties

For centuries the Ojibwa/Chippewa Indians have harvested wild rice in the marshes of Minnesota. Wild rice has been a part of their culture since the very beginning. Even today, many Chippewa Indians depend on the sales of their hand-harvested wild rice. In 1977, Minnesota decided to make wild rice its official state grain in order to help promote it. We thought we'd help them out even further by sharing this amazing recipe. You don't want to miss out!

Makes 16

Ingredients

½ cup mayonnaise

2 eggs

2 teaspoons ground cumin

1 teaspoon garlic powder

1 teaspoon salt

½ teaspoon black pepper

¼ teaspoon crushed red pepper

3 cups cooked wild rice, chilled (see Tip)

¾ cup coarsely chopped mushrooms

¾ cup panko bread crumbs

2 tablespoons vegetable oil

Preparation

1 In a large bowl, combine mayonnaise, eggs, cumin, garlic powder, salt, black pepper, and crushed red pepper; mix well. Add rice, mushrooms, and bread crumbs; mix until thoroughly combined.

2 Using about a ¼ cup mixture for each, form into 16 equal patties.

3 In a large skillet over medium heat, heat oil until hot. Cook patties in batches 3 to 4 minutes per side or until crispy and golden brown. Drain on a paper towel-lined platter. Serve piping hot.

Test Kitchen Tip: *Since there are many brands of wild rice at the market, we suggest you refer to the package for cooking directions. You will need 6 (½-cup) servings. Let the cooked rice chill before using it to make these amazing rice patties.*

Lone Star Spätzle

While there are German-Americans living all across the country, you might be surprised to learn that one of the most unique German-American towns can be found in the state of Texas. The city of Fredericksburg was founded by German settlers in 1846 and is a popular tourist destination that's full of history. If you ever find yourself in this town, be sure to stop by one of the many restaurants serving up authentic German fare, so you can try some of the classics, like spätzle!

Serves 6

Ingredients

3 cups all-purpose flour

½ teaspoon baking powder

2 teaspoons salt, divided

½ teaspoon black pepper

4 eggs, beaten

2 cups water

½ stick butter

1 teaspoon chopped fresh parsley

Preparation

1 In a large bowl, combine flour, baking powder, 1-½ teaspoons salt, and the pepper; mix well. Add eggs and water; mix with a wooden spoon until smooth.

2 Over high heat, bring a large pot of water to a rolling boil; add remaining ½ teaspoon salt. In batches, drizzle the batter from a wide-slotted spoon into the boiling water. When the spätzle (the cooked batter) float to the top of the water, remove them with a another slotted spoon or drain in a colander.

3 In a large skillet over medium-low heat, melt butter. Add spätzle and parsley, and cook 4 to 5 minutes or until heated through.

Frog Eye Salad

Acini di pepe is a type of small round pasta that's a must-have ingredient in Frog Eye Salad, and yes, it's available in most supermarkets. After all, it's the pasta that gives this dish its name, since some people happen to think it looks like frog eyes. This dish is a cross between a pasta salad and a fruit salad, which basically makes it okay to serve as either a side dish or dessert. In Utah and its surrounding states, this is considered a childhood favorite.

Serves 12

Ingredients

½ (16-ounce) box acini de pepe pasta

1 (20-ounce) can pineapple tidbits, drained, with about 1 cup juice reserved

½ cup sugar

1 tablespoon all-purpose flour

¼ teaspoon salt

1 egg, beaten

1 teaspoon lemon juice

1-½ cups miniature marshmallows

1 cup shredded coconut

1 (15-ounce) can mandarin oranges, drained

1 (8-ounce) container frozen whipped topping, thawed

Preparation

1 Cook pasta according to package directions; drain. Rinse under cold water, drain again, and let cool.

2 In a saucepan over medium heat, combine reserved pineapple juice, the sugar, flour, salt, and egg. Cook, stirring constantly, until thickened and mixture is smooth. Remove from heat and stir in lemon juice. Let cool.

3 In a large bowl, combine pasta and cooled pineapple juice mixture. Stir in pineapple tidbits, marshmallows, and coconut. Gently fold in mandarin oranges and whipped topping. Enjoy right away or refrigerate until ready to serve.

American Indian Fry Bread

Fry bread is a type of fried dough. It's a traditional food for many American Indians, especially the Navajo. To them, it is a symbolic food with a memorable role in their history. There are lots of different ways to make fry bread, and everyone has their preference. For example, some folks make a hole in theirs, which they call a "belly button," in order to keep the dough from bubbling up too much. Hole or not, fry bread is pretty darn tasty and versatile!

Makes 8

Ingredients

4 cups all-purpose flour

1 tablespoon baking powder

½ teaspoon salt

1-½ cups warm water

2 cups vegetable shortening

Preparation

1 In a large bowl, combine flour, baking powder, and salt; mix well. Stir in warm water until combined.

2 Knead dough until soft. Shape dough into 8 equal balls and place in a 9- x 13-inch baking dish. Cover with a towel and let rest 10 minutes.

3 Using a rolling pin, roll out each dough ball to form a 5-inch circle. With your finger, make a small hole in the center of each circle.

4 In a large skillet over medium heat, heat vegetable shortening until hot, but not smoking. Fry 1 dough circle 2 to 3 minutes per side or until golden brown; drain on a paper towel-lined platter. Repeat with remaining dough.

Did You Know? *Fry bread is served all over the Southwest—at fairs, festivals, and pow-wow's (social gatherings). It is eaten as-is, topped with a little butter or honey, or sprinkled with a cinnamon-sugar mixture. It's also used as the base for Indian Tacos. To make these, just load up your fry bread with ground beef, beans, and your favorite taco toppings.*

Alabama Fire Crackers

Whether you make these for a potluck, picnic, game day, or special occasion, you can bet they're going to be a hit. Every bite is full of flavor and packs just the right amount of heat. And not only are they easy to throw together, but they're made the day before you need them, which means you'll have one less thing to worry about on the day of.

Makes about 7 dozen

Ingredients

1 (1-ounce) packet dry ranch dressing mix

1 tablespoon crushed red pepper

½ teaspoon garlic powder

½ teaspoon onion powder

¼ teaspoon black pepper

¾ cup vegetable oil

2 sleeves (½ box) saltine crackers

Preparation

1 In a 2-gallon resealable plastic bag, (see Note) combine dressing mix, red pepper flakes, garlic powder, onion powder, and black pepper; mix well. Add oil and mix well.

2 Place crackers in bag, seal, and turn bag over several times until crackers are evenly coated. Do this gently to avoid breaking the crackers. Allow to sit about 1 hour before turning again. Let bag sit overnight. Store crackers in bag or an airtight container until ready to serve.

Note: If you don't have any 2-gallon bags, you can split the seasoning mix and crackers into 2 (1-gallon) bags.

Serving Suggestion: You can enjoy these all by themselves or serve them alongside a bowl of hearty chili, like we did on page 134. Actually, you can serve them alongside anything – they're that good!

Gorgeous sunsets can happen anywhere. We were lucky to see this one in Amish Country in Lancaster County, PA. See page 230 for our Amish Shoofly Pie!

Howard put on his boots and cowboy hat to experience a true taste of the West. Yeehaw - don't forget the cornbread!

Here's a tip - always stop at the roadside stands when you're traveling. It's the best way to taste freshly-picked produce. These California strawberries were so juicy!

We always obey the road signs. So, when we saw this one, we made sure to stop and sample the amazing, homemade root beer before continuing our travels.

Patty and Kelly are pretty great at finding the dessert tents at farmer's markets!

Delectable Desserts

Mississippi Mud Pie

No one knows for sure what the real story behind the mud pie is, but we like the one that claims that the pie was named after the muddy banks of the Mississippi. One thing that everyone can agree on is that this dessert is a chocoholic's dream. Whether you're east, west, north, or south of the Mississippi, we think you'll enjoy every bite of this rich and heavenly pie.

Serves 8

Ingredients

28 chocolate sandwich cookies

½ stick butter, melted

⅔ cup sweetened condensed milk

1 cup semisweet chocolate chips

1 (4-serving-size) package cook & serve chocolate pudding and pie filling

2 cups milk

1 (8-ounce) container frozen whipped topping, thawed

¼ cup chopped pecans

Preparation

1   Place cookies in a food processor and process until finely ground. Place in a medium bowl, add butter, and mix well. Press cookie mixture firmly into deep dish pie plate forming a crust. Refrigerate until firm.

2   Meanwhile, in a small saucepan over medium-low heat, combine condensed milk and chocolate chips and heat 4 to 5 minutes or until chocolate is melted, stirring occasionally. Evenly spoon over pie crust and set aside.

3   In a medium saucepan over medium heat, combine pudding mix and milk, and cook until mixture thickens and comes to a boil, stirring occasionally. Let pudding mixture cool 5 minutes. Spoon pudding evenly over chocolate layer and refrigerate 1 hour.

4   Top pie with whipped topping and garnish with nuts. Refrigerate at least 3 hours or until ready to serve.

All-American Apple Pie

No dessert is considered more American than apple pie. It's made all over the country in hundreds of different ways. Even the way it's served differs from place to place (some people like a scoop of ice cream, while others prefer a slice of cheddar cheese!). Over the years we've come up with our fair share of apple pies, but this one is truly one for the books. Just wait till you taste a slice!

Serves 8

Ingredients

- ¾ cup plus 1 teaspoon sugar, divided
- 3 tablespoons all-purpose flour
- 1 teaspoon ground cinnamon
- ½ teaspoon ground nutmeg
- 6 assorted apples, peeled and thinly sliced (see Tip)
- 1 tablespoon butter, cut into pieces
- 1 (14.1-ounce) package refrigerated rolled pie crust
- 1 teaspoon milk

Preparation

1 Preheat oven to 400 degrees F.

2 In a large bowl, combine ¾ cup sugar, the flour, cinnamon, and nutmeg; mix well. Add apples and butter, and toss until evenly coated.

3 Unroll 1 pie crust and place in a 9-inch deep dish pie plate, pressing crust firmly against pie plate. Spoon apple mixture into crust, then place remaining crust over apples. Pinch edges together to seal, then flute. Using a knife, cut four 1-inch slits in top. Brush milk over crust and sprinkle with remaining 1 teaspoon sugar.

4 Place on a baking sheet and bake 50 to 55 minutes or until crust is golden. Allow to cool one hour before serving.

Test Kitchen Tip: To take advantage of all of the great apples in each region of the country, we suggest combining a few different varieties in your pie. That way you get a mixture of firm and soft and tart and sweet.

Sunshine State Key Lime Pie

Who would've thought that such a small fruit could add such an intense flavor to a pie? Key limes, which are originally named after the Florida Keys, are citrusy, tart, and tasty. In a Key lime pie, they help to balance the sweetness from the condensed milk, making for a delicious flavor combo. While they're made all over Florida, they're especially famous in the Keys where you can find this rich and creamy treat served in practically every restaurant.

Serves 8

Ingredients

1 cup graham cracker crumbs

5 tablespoons butter, melted

⅓ cup granulated sugar

3 egg yolks

1-½ teaspoons grated lime zest

1 (14-ounce) can sweetened condensed milk

⅔ cup Key lime juice

1 cup heavy cream

3 tablespoons confectioners' sugar

Preparation

1 Preheat oven to 350 degrees F. Coat bottom of a 9-inch pie plate with cooking spray.

2 In a medium bowl, combine graham cracker crumbs, butter, and granulated sugar; mix well. Press mixture over bottom and up sides of pie plate to form a crust; set aside.

3 In a medium bowl, with an electric mixer on medium speed, beat egg yolks and lime zest 2 minutes. Gradually add sweetened condensed milk and continue beating 3 minutes. Reduce speed to low and gradually beat in lime juice until combined. Pour filling into crust.

4 Bake 10 minutes or until the center is firm. Remove from oven and let cool on a wire rack, then cover and chill at least 4 hours before serving.

5 When ready to serve, in a medium bowl, beat heavy cream and confectioners' sugar until stiff peaks form. Dollop on pie and serve.

Did You Know? A Key lime pie should be pale yellow in color and not bright green. That's because a ripe Key lime is typically yellowish-green on the outside with pale yellow juice when squeezed. The egg yolks also play a role in keeping the filling yellow. If you can't find fresh Key limes, you can find bottled Key lime juice in your market right alongside regular lime juice.

Chocolate Bourbon Pecan Pie

Bourbon whiskey was born in Kentucky, and the state is still one of the world's largest suppliers of this spirit. So it should come as no surprise to learn that one of the most popular pies of the state features that ol' Kentucky bourbon taste that everyone loves. It's traditionally served at Derby parties alongside a refreshing Mint Julep, but we think this crunchy, gooey, and chocolaty pie deserves a place at your dessert table year-round.

Serves 8

Ingredients

1 refrigerated rolled pie crust (from a 14.1-ounce package)

½ cup firmly packed brown sugar

2 tablespoons all-purpose flour

¼ teaspoon salt

1 cup light corn syrup

3 tablespoons bourbon

3 tablespoons butter, melted

1-½ teaspoons vanilla extract

3 eggs

1-¼ cups coarsely chopped pecans

1 cup semisweet chocolate chips

Preparation

1 Preheat oven to 350 degrees F. Place pie crust in a deep dish pie plate and flute edges.

2 In a large bowl, combine brown sugar, flour, and salt; mix well. Add corn syrup, bourbon, butter, vanilla, and eggs; mix until thoroughly combined. Stir in pecans and chocolate chips. Pour mixture into pie shell.

3 Bake 45 to 50 minutes or until set. Let cool, then refrigerate 4 hours or until ready to serve.

*Did You Know? The Mint Julep has been the traditional drink of the Kentucky Derby for almost a century. To make a **Mint Julep**, all you do is add a teaspoon of sugar into a 12-ounce glass, along with a couple of sprigs of mint; muddle (crush) until mashed together. Fill glass with ice. Add 3 ounces of Kentucky bourbon, stir well, and garnish with a sprig of mint.*

Traditional Amish Shoofly Pie

There are a couple of different stories about where this pie got its name, but our favorite is the one that paints a picture of bakers swatting away the flies cooling on their window sills. ("Shoo, fly!"). You'll discover that this pie has an unmistakable taste to it - it's molasses. Molasses is a favorite ingredient in Pennsylvania Dutch country, which is where this pie got its start and where it continues to be a beloved tradition.

Serves 8

Ingredients

1 refrigerated rolled pie crust (from a 14.1-ounce package)

1-¼ cups all-purpose flour

¾ cup dark brown sugar

3 tablespoons cold butter

¼ teaspoon salt

¾ cup boiling water

1 teaspoon baking soda

1 cup molasses

1 egg

Preparation

1 Preheat oven to 350 degrees F. Place pie crust in a 9-inch pie plate and flute edges.

2 In a medium bowl, combine flour, brown sugar, butter, and salt; mix well until crumbly.

3 In another medium bowl, mix boiling water and baking soda. Add molasses and egg; mix well. Stir in half the flour mixture and pour into pie crust. Top with remaining half of flour mixture.

4 Bake 40 to 45 minutes or until crust is golden and center of filling is still slightly jiggly. (Pie will firm up as it sits.) Cool completely before cutting.

Test Kitchen Tip: When it comes to molasses, you either love it or...well, let's just say, you don't. If trying it for the first time, we suggest making this pie with a lighter molasses. It'll be a bit sweeter and not as bitter as blackstrap molasses, which has the most intense flavor.

Not-What-You-Think Possum Pie

Before you start to get all squeamish, we feel that we should explain the reason behind this pie's name. This Arkansas specialty is named so because it's said to "play possum." In other words, it's sort of difficult to tell what's going on just by looking at it. That's why it's important to dig in right away! Once you do, you'll discover that there's lots of layers to love - from crunchy to creamy. One taste and you'll be telling everyone all about it!

Serves 8

Ingredients

1 cup all-purpose flour

1 cup finely chopped pecans

1 stick butter, melted

4 ounces cream cheese, softened

½ cup confectioners' sugar

1 teaspoon vanilla extract

1 (8-ounce) container frozen whipped topping, thawed, divided

1 (4-serving-size) package instant chocolate fudge pudding and pie filling

1-½ cups milk

Preparation

1 Preheat oven to 350 degrees F.

2 In a medium bowl, combine flour, pecans, and butter; mix with a fork until thoroughly combined. Press mixture into a 9-inch deep dish pie plate, forming a crust.

3 Bake 15 to 20 minutes or until crust starts to brown. Remove from oven and cool.

4 In a medium bowl, beat cream cheese, confectioners' sugar, and vanilla until smooth. Add 1 cup whipped topping and mix until thoroughly combined. Spread mixture evenly over crust.

5 In a medium bowl, whisk pudding mix and milk until thickened. Spread pudding mixture over cream cheese layer. Top with remaining whipped topping. Refrigerate 4 hours or until ready to serve.

Fancy it Up: Since we eat with our eyes, we suggest topping this with a couple of tablespoons of chopped pecans and some shaved chocolate.

Hoosier Sugar Cream Pie

Indiana's official state pie dates back to the early pioneer days. It's known for being a fairly simple pie with two must-have ingredients: sugar and cream. Custard-like and just a little jiggly, this pie has always been famous for being a great "out of the cupboard" dessert, since there's nothing fancy about it. It's a great change-of-pace from a fruit pie and a real "Hoosier" favorite.

Serves 8

Ingredients

1 refrigerated rolled pie crust (from a 14.1-ounce package)

½ cup all-purpose flour

½ cup light brown sugar

1 cup plus 1 tablespoon granulated sugar, divided

¾ teaspoon ground cinnamon, divided

¼ teaspoon ground nutmeg

½ teaspoon salt

1-½ cups heavy cream

1 cup half-and-half

2 teaspoons vanilla extract

Preparation

1 Preheat oven to 375 degrees F. Unroll pie crust and place in a 9-inch pie plate. Create a criss-cross pattern around the edge with a fork and set aside.

2 In a large bowl, combine flour, brown sugar, 1 cup granulated sugar, ½ teaspoon cinnamon, the nutmeg, and salt. Add heavy cream, half-and-half, and vanilla; stir until well mixed. Pour into pie crust.

3 Bake 45 to 50 minutes or until center is set; let cool, then refrigerate at least 6 hours or until chilled.

4 In a small bowl, mix remaining 1 tablespoon sugar and ¼ teaspoon cinnamon; sprinkle over pie before serving.

Serving Suggestion: *For an extra burst of flavor, grate some fresh nutmeg over the top!*

Prize-Winning Lane Cake

This cake dates way back to the late 19th century, when it was created by Emma Rylander Lane, an Alabama native, who won first place at a baking competition. It became very popular in the South and continues to be a favorite today. While cooks have made some changes to the original recipe, some things still hold true. A Lane Cake is always a layered cake filled with dried fruits and nuts, and a bit of liquor, too.

Serves 12

Ingredients

8 eggs, separated, with 4 egg whites reserved (see Note)

1 package white cake mix

¼ teaspoon ground nutmeg

1 cup water

¼ cup vegetable oil

1-¼ cups sugar

1 stick butter

½ cup brandy

1 teaspoon vanilla extract

1 cup chopped raisins

1 cup shredded coconut

1 cup chopped pecans

½ cup chopped maraschino cherries, drained well

1 (16-ounce) container white frosting

Note: You can either discard the extra 4 egg whites or use them for another purpose.

Preparation

1 Preheat oven to 350 degrees F. Coat 2 (8-inch) round cake pans with cooking spray.

2 In a medium bowl with an electric mixer, beat 4 egg whites until stiff peaks form. In a large bowl, beat cake mix, nutmeg, water, and oil until smooth. Fold egg whites into cake mixture. Divide batter evenly between cake pans.

3 Bake 22 to 25 minutes or until toothpick inserted in center comes out clean. Let cool 10 minutes, then invert onto wire racks to cool completely. Cut cakes in half horizontally, forming four layers.

4 In a medium saucepan, whisk egg yolks and sugar until smooth. Add butter and cook over medium heat 6 to 8 minutes or until thick enough to coat the back of a spoon, stirring constantly. Remove from heat and stir in brandy and vanilla. Add raisins, coconut, pecans, and cherries; mix well.

5 Place one cake layer on a serving platter and spread with one-third of filling. Repeat layers two more times and top with fourth cake layer. Frost top and sides with frosting. Cover loosely and refrigerate until ready to serve.

"Oopsy!" Gooey Butter Cake

Not all mistakes end in disaster, and the proof of that is right on this page. In both popular versions of the gooey butter cake story, it seems that the result came from someone's "oops!" In one, a baker added too much butter. In another, a baker used the "wrong" kind of butter. The good news is, no one complained about this mishap then, and no one is complaining now. Gooey butter cake has become a St. Louis staple, and we love every gooey bite!

Serves 12

Ingredients

CRUST
1 cup all-purpose flour

3 tablespoons granulated sugar

6 tablespoons butter, softened

FILLING
1-¼ cups granulated sugar

1-½ sticks butter, softened

1-½ teaspoons vanilla extract

¼ teaspoon salt

¼ cup light corn syrup

1 egg

1 cup all-purpose flour

1 (5-ounce) can evaporated milk

Confectioners' sugar for sprinkling

Preparation

1 Preheat oven to 350 degrees F.

2 In a medium bowl, combine all crust ingredients; use a fork to mix until crumbly. Press mixture into bottom of a 9-inch square baking dish. (See Note.)

3 To make filling, in a large bowl, combine granulated sugar, butter, vanilla, and salt until creamy. Beat in corn syrup and egg until combined. Slowly add flour and evaporated milk, beating just until combined. Pour filling into crust and spread evenly.

4 Bake 35 to 40 minutes or until cake is almost firm in center when gently shaken. (See Tip.) Let cool, then sprinkle with confectioners' sugar.

Note: If you don't have a 9-inch square baking dish, it's ok to use an 8-inch one, just increase baking time to 40 to 45 minutes.

Test Kitchen Tip: The good old toothpick doneness test doesn't work for this cake as the center is gooey even when it's done, which is just what we want!

New York Deli-Style Cheesecake

Some of the best cheesecakes in the country can be found in delis all around New York. It's also no surprise that when most people are asked to name popular cheesecakes the "New York Cheesecake" has a way of making their lists. The crazy thing is, there's nothing fancy about it! It's basically just a dense cake made with sour cream and cream cheese, which makes it extra-smooth. Whatever the reason for its popularity, we're happy it stuck around long enough to become a national favorite.

Serves 12

Ingredients

- 1-½ cups graham cracker crumbs
- 1-¼ cups plus 2 tablespoons sugar, divided
- 1 stick butter, melted
- 4 (8-ounce) packages cream cheese, softened
- 3 eggs
- 1 cup sour cream
- ½ cup all-purpose flour
- 1 tablespoon vanilla extract

Preparation

1 Preheat oven to 350 degrees F.

2 In a medium bowl, combine graham cracker crumbs, 2 tablespoons sugar, and butter; mix well. Press crumb mixture into bottom of a 9-inch springform pan; set aside.

3 In a large bowl, beat cream cheese and remaining 1-¼ cups sugar until smooth. Beat in remaining ingredients just until combined. Spoon batter onto crust.

4 Bake 55 minutes. (Cheesecake will be jiggly in center.) Turn off oven; leave cheesecake in oven 1 hour. Place on counter and let cool 2 to 3 hours at room temperature. Cover and chill at least 6 hours before serving.

Test Kitchen Tip: *Cooling the cake slowly in the oven and then on the counter will help prevent it from cracking. It's a good idea to set a timer during the cooling part of this so you don't forget about it and leave it in the oven all night. Yikes!*

Simply Sweet Strawberry Shortcake

When Delaware declared the strawberry its official state fruit in 2010, they made it clear that their strawberries were "bred for taste" instead of size or shelf life. While there are plenty of great strawberry desserts to choose from, we decided to follow their lead and keep things simple with a shortcake that's "made for strawberries." There's no fuss and no fanciness, just a dessert that's "berry good."

Serves 9

Ingredients

1 stick butter, softened

1 cup plus 1 tablespoon sugar, divided

1 egg

1 teaspoon vanilla extract

2 cups all-purpose flour

1 tablespoon baking powder

½ teaspoon salt

1 cup milk

4 cups sliced fresh strawberries

Whipped cream for garnish

Preparation

1 Preheat oven to 350 degrees F. Coat a 9-inch square baking dish with cooking spray. (See Tip.)

2 In a large bowl with an electric mixer, beat butter, ¾ cup sugar, the egg, and vanilla until creamy. Add flour, baking powder, and salt; mix well. Slowly beat in milk until smooth. Spoon mixture into baking dish and sprinkle with 1 tablespoon sugar.

3 Bake 25 to 30 minutes or until toothpick inserted in center comes out clean. Let cool.

4 Before serving, in a medium bowl, combine strawberries and remaining ¼ cup sugar; mix well. Cover and refrigerate at least 30 minutes. When ready to serve, cut shortcake into squares, and top with strawberries and whipped cream.

Test Kitchen Tip: *If you don't have a 9-inch baking dish, you can use an 8-inch square baking dish. However, the baking time will be 35 to 40 minutes.*

Texas-Sized Sheet Cake

Texas is pretty big; it's the second largest state in the country (after Alaska). So what if you were asked to make a cake that lived up to the old saying, "Everything's bigger in Texas"? Would you make a really tall layer cake or a super-sized sheet cake? We went with the second option. This double chocolate sheet cake is big enough to feed all of your friends, and maybe some of their friends, too. The homemade frosting even features another Texas favorite - pecans!

Serves 15

Ingredients

2 sticks butter

1 cup water

⅓ cup cocoa powder

2 cups all-purpose flour

2 cups granulated sugar

2 eggs

¾ cup sour cream

1 teaspoon baking soda

½ teaspoon salt

FROSTING

6 tablespoons butter

⅓ cup milk

3 tablespoons cocoa powder

3 cups confectioners' sugar

1 teaspoon vanilla extract

½ cup chopped pecans, toasted

Preparation

1 Preheat oven to 350 degrees F. Coat a 10- x 15-inch rimmed baking sheet with cooking spray.

2 In a small saucepan over low heat, combine 2 sticks butter, the water, and ⅓ cup cocoa powder; heat until butter is melted, stirring occasionally. Remove from heat and pour into a large bowl to cool. Add flour, granulated sugar, eggs, sour cream, baking soda, and salt; beat until well combined. Pour into baking sheet.

3 Bake 25 minutes or until a toothpick inserted in center comes out clean; let cool.

4 In a small saucepan over low heat, make frosting by melting 6 tablespoons butter with the milk and 3 tablespoons cocoa powder. Remove from heat and place in a large bowl. Gradually beat in confectioners' sugar and vanilla until smooth. Frost cake, then sprinkle with pecans.

Tres Leches Poke Cake

"Tres leches" is Spanish for "three milks." It was introduced to the U.S. by immigrants from countries in South and Central America, as well as the Caribbean. Today, it's popular in many states with a large Hispanic population, including New Mexico. If you're not familiar with it, you're in for a treat. This spongy cake is soaked with a mixture of three milks and topped with heavenly, homemade whipped cream. Every bite will have you asking for more.

Serves 15

Ingredients

1-¼ cups all-purpose flour

1 teaspoon baking powder

¼ teaspoon salt

5 eggs

1-¼ cups sugar, divided

1 stick butter, melted

3 teaspoons vanilla extract, divided

1 (14-ounce) can condensed milk

1 (12-ounce) can evaporated milk

3 cups heavy cream, divided

¼ cup rum

Fancy it Up: You can serve this as-is or garnish the top of each slice with fresh or canned fruit.

Preparation

1 Preheat oven to 325 degrees F. Coat a 9- x 13-inch baking dish with cooking spray.

2 In a medium bowl, combine flour, baking powder, and salt; mix well and set aside. In a large bowl, beat eggs until frothy. Slowly beat in 1 cup sugar, the butter, and 1 teaspoon vanilla. Add flour mixture slowly and mix just until combined. Pour batter evenly into baking dish. Bake 30 to 35 minutes or until toothpick inserted in center comes out clean. Let cool.

3 Meanwhile, in a medium saucepan over low heat, combine condensed milk, evaporated milk, 1 cup heavy cream, the rum, and 1 teaspoon vanilla until warm. Remove from heat and set aside.

4 Using a fork or skewer, poke holes all over top of cake. Pour milk mixture evenly over top of cake and into holes. Cover and refrigerate 4 hours or overnight.

5 Before serving, in a large bowl with an electric mixer, beat the remaining 2 cups heavy cream, the ¼ cup sugar, and the 1 teaspoon vanilla until stiff peaks form. Spread whipped cream evenly over top of cake. Refrigerate until ready to serve.

Upside-Down Cranberry Bog Cake

Not all farmers drive tractors and tend to cattle. For many farmers in the New England area, a typical day involves throwing on a pair of rubber waders and going knee-deep into a cranberry bog. The Northeastern region of the country is known far and wide for its production of these small and tart berries. While they can be eaten fresh, their tartness is usually preferred in sweet desserts like this one.

Serves 12

Ingredients

1 stick butter, melted, divided

2 cups fresh (or frozen and thawed) cranberries

½ cup walnuts, coarsely chopped

⅓ cup plus ¾ cup sugar

2 eggs

1 teaspoon vanilla extract

1 cup all-purpose flour

¼ teaspoon salt

Preparation

1 Preheat oven to 350 degrees F. Pour 2 tablespoons butter into bottom of an 8-inch square baking dish. Place cranberries evenly over bottom of dish. Sprinkle with walnuts, then with ⅓ cup sugar; set aside.

2 In a medium bowl, beat eggs, vanilla, and remaining ¾ cup sugar until creamy. Gradually beat in flour and salt. Add remaining butter and beat until smooth. Pour batter evenly over walnuts.

3 Bake 35 to 40 minutes, or until golden and toothpick inserted in center comes out clean. Let cool 10 minutes on a wire rack. Run a knife around edges of baking dish to loosen. Carefully invert onto serving platter. Serve warm or at room temperature.

Test Kitchen Tip: There's a pretty good chance that you'll make this around the holidays and you should have no problem finding fresh cranberries. However, it's so good, you'll probably want to make it year-round, so buy a few extra bags of fresh cranberries and pop them in the freezer.

Wonderful Whoopie Pies

Folks in Maine must have a real sweet tooth, since they have both an official state dessert (blueberry pie) and an official state treat (whoopie pies). While we have to give credit to the Amish for the original recipe, Maine has really taken this treat over the top. Not only do whoopie pies tend to be a little larger in Maine, but the state holds an annual festival to celebrate their favorite stuffed sweet. Enjoy it like they do with a tall glass of milk!

Makes 10

Ingredients

1 package chocolate fudge cake mix

1 (4-serving-size) package instant chocolate pudding and pie filling mix

½ cup all-purpose flour

1 cup water

⅓ cup vegetable oil

3 eggs

2 cups vegetable shortening

2 cups confectioners' sugar

2 cups marshmallow crème

1 teaspoon vanilla extract

Preparation

1 Preheat oven to 350 degrees F. Coat 2 baking sheets with cooking spray.

2 In a large bowl with an electric mixer, beat cake mix, pudding mix, flour, water, oil, and eggs until thoroughly combined. Drop ¼ cup batter per cookie onto baking sheets.

3 Bake 13 to 15 minutes or until toothpick comes out clean. Let cool slightly, then remove to a wire rack to cool completely.

4 In a large bowl with an electric mixer, beat shortening and confectioners' sugar until creamy. Add marshmallow crème and vanilla, and mix until smooth. Spoon filling evenly onto flat side of half the cookies. Place remaining cookies over cream filling and push down slightly, forming sandwiches.

Luck o' the Irish Blarney Stones

St. Patrick's Day is a pretty big deal in Emmetsburg, Iowa. The city has a rich Irish history; it's one of the few places in the U.S. that's home to a piece of the original Blarney Stone from Ireland! To celebrate their heritage, folks from all over the city (and state) bake up these sweet treats. We're not sure if eating them has the same effect as kissing the stone, but we're willing to bet that sharing them will make you seem more charming.

Makes 32

Ingredients

CAKE

1 cup all-purpose flour

1-½ teaspoons baking powder

¼ teaspoon salt

4 eggs, separated

1 cup granulated sugar

½ cup boiling water

1 teaspoon vanilla extract

FROSTING

2 sticks butter, softened

3 cups confectioners' sugar

1 tablespoon milk

1-½ teaspoons vanilla extract

1 cup salted peanuts, finely crushed

16 maraschino cherries, halved and drained well

Preparation

1. Preheat oven to 350 degrees F. Coat a 9- x 13-inch baking dish with cooking spray.

2. In a bowl, combine flour, baking powder, and salt; set aside. In another bowl with an electric mixer, beat egg whites until stiff; set aside. In a large bowl with an electric mixer, beat egg yolks until thick; gradually add granulated sugar, beating continuously. Add water, alternating with flour mixture. Add vanilla until well combined, then fold in egg whites. Pour batter into baking dish.

3. Bake 25 to 30 minutes or until toothpick inserted in center comes out clean; let cool 10 minutes then remove to a wire rack to cool completely.

4. Meanwhile, in a large bowl with an electric mixer, beat frosting ingredients until well combined.

5. Cut cake into 1-½-inch squares, frost tops and sides, roll in peanuts, and garnish each with half a cherry.

Test Kitchen Tip: *Don't have time to frost each individual piece? Just frost the top of the cake before cutting, sprinkle with peanuts, and top with cherries.*

Wisconsin State Fair Cream Puffs

Every year, people line up, drive up, or order delivery for cream puffs from the Wisconsin State Fair. The fair sells thousands of these daily, and the cream puffs are not available outside of fair dates. Well, at least that used to be the case. With our recipe, you can enjoy your favorite fluffy puffs any time, whether you're too far from the fair location or you're craving this famous dessert out of season. Make sure you use two hands - these are pretty big!

Makes 8

Ingredients

1 cup water

½ stick butter

¼ teaspoon salt

1 cup all-purpose flour

4 eggs, at room temperature

1 egg yolk

2 tablespoons milk

2 cups (1 pint) heavy cream

⅓ cup confectioners' sugar, plus extra for sprinkling

2 teaspoons vanilla extract

Preparation

1. Preheat oven to 400 degrees F. In a medium saucepan over medium-high heat, bring water, butter, and salt to a boil. Add flour all at once and stir quickly until mixture forms a ball; remove from heat. Add 1 egg and mix well with a wooden spoon to blend. Add remaining eggs one at a time, beating well after each addition. (Each egg must be completely blended in before the next egg is added.) As you beat mixture, it will change from an almost-curdled to a smooth appearance. When it is smooth, spoon 8 mounds of dough onto a large rimmed baking sheet.

2. In a small bowl, combine the egg yolk and milk; mix well and brush over dough.

3. Bake 25 to 30 minutes or until golden. Remove to a wire rack to cool completely.

4. Meanwhile, in a large bowl with an electric mixer on medium speed, beat heavy cream until soft peaks form. Add ⅓ cup confectioners' sugar and the vanilla, and beat until stiff peaks form. Cut top third off each pastry puff and fill with equal amounts of whipped cream mixture. Replace tops and sprinkle with confectioners' sugar. Serve immediately or cover and chill until ready to serve.

Test Kitchen Tip: For a sure way to get perfect whipped cream, chill the bowl and beaters before whipping the cream, and make sure not to overbeat it

Homemade Buckeyes

If you ever find yourself in Ohio, make it a point to check out some buckeye trees. The nuts that grow on these trees inspired the name for this popular peanut butter and chocolate candy. It's said that these were created by a woman whose husband was a big Ohio State football fan. Coincidentally, buckeyes are still an Ohio game day favorite and are made in large batches for everyone to munch on while cheering for their home team.

Makes 30

Ingredients

1 cup smooth peanut butter

1 stick butter, softened

2-½ cups confectioners' sugar

1 cup semisweet chocolate chips

1 tablespoon vegetable shortening

Preparation

1 In a large bowl, combine peanut butter and butter; mix until smooth. Gradually add confectioners' sugar, stirring until thoroughly mixed. Form mixture into 1-inch balls, place on a wax paper-lined baking sheet, and chill 1 hour.

2 In a microwave-safe bowl, microwave chocolate chips and shortening 1 minute; stir. Continue to microwave in 10-second intervals until chocolate is completely melted and smooth. Stick a toothpick in the center of each peanut butter ball and dip each three-quarters of the way into the chocolate mixture, coating all but the top. Place on baking sheet and remove toothpick. Using your finger, fill in the hole left by the toothpick.

3 After dipping all the peanut butter balls, cover and chill or freeze until ready to serve.

Test Kitchen Tip: We found that the easiest way to make sure that all of our peanut butter balls are the same size is to scoop them with a small ice cream scoop. If you don't have one, pick one up as they're also great for scooping out cookie dough.

North Dakota's Christmas Cookies

During Christmas, it's traditional for families to make recipes that have been passed down through the generations. In North Dakota, where there is a large Scandinavian population, you'll find lots of people baking these rich and buttery cookies, known as berlinerkranser. They look great on a cookie platter and are melt-in-your-mouth good, so give them a try when you're craving something sweet.

Makes about 22

Ingredients

2 sticks butter, softened

½ cup confectioners' sugar

1 egg, separated

1 hard-boiled egg yolk, grated

1-½ teaspoons vanilla extract

2-¼ cups all-purpose flour

½ cup sugar cubes, coarsely crushed

Test Kitchen Tip: It's best to brush these with egg and sugar them on a cutting board or another tray that you're not baking on. If you brush these on the baking sheet that you bake them on, they'll stick.

Preparation

1 In a large bowl, beat butter and confectioners' sugar until creamy. Beat in raw egg yolk, grated egg yolk, and the vanilla. Add flour; mix well. Cover and chill 1 hour.

2 Preheat oven to 325 degrees F. Line baking sheets with parchment paper.

3 Using about 1 tablespoon of dough for each cookie, roll each into a 6-inch rope. (Work with a small amount of dough at a time, keeping the rest refrigerated until needed.) Form each rope into a ribbon shape, overlapping about 1 inch from ends.

4 In a small bowl, lightly beat egg white. Brush dough lightly with egg white and sprinkle with crushed sugar cubes. Place cookies on baking sheets.

5 Bake 15 to 18 minutes or until golden. Cool 1 minute, then remove carefully to a wire rack to cool completely. (They must be removed while hot or they may break apart.)

Mackinac Island Chocolate Walnut Fudge

Mackinac Island may be just a small island at the northern end of Michigan, but that hasn't stopped it from becoming known as the fudge capital of the United States. The island is home to several fudge shops, all of which sell many different fudge flavor varieties. However, it's been said that a local favorite is still plain old chocolate. Inspired by all things fudgy, we came up with our own homemade version that we think is pretty darn good.

Makes 5 dozen pieces

Ingredients

1 stick plus 1 teaspoon butter, divided

½ cup milk

¾ cup granulated sugar

½ cup brown sugar

⅛ teaspoon salt

1 teaspoon vanilla extract

2 cups confectioners' sugar

½ cup cocoa powder

½ cup coarsely chopped walnuts

Preparation

1 Lightly grease the bottom of an 8-inch square baking dish with 1 teaspoon butter.

2 In a medium saucepan over medium heat, combine the remaining 1 stick butter, the milk, granulated sugar, brown sugar, and salt; bring to a boil and continue to boil 6 minutes, stirring constantly.

3 Remove from heat; add vanilla, confectioners' sugar, and cocoa powder. Beat with an electric mixer until smooth; stir in walnuts.

4 Spoon mixture into baking dish and refrigerate 1 hour or until firm. Cut into pieces and store in an airtight container.

Test Kitchen Tip: The best way to store fudge is to keep it in an airtight container at room temperature for a couple of weeks. If you refrigerate it, there's a good chance that it'll become gritty as the sugar begins to crystallize.

Georgia Peach Cinnamon Cobbler

Georgia knows a thing or two about peaches. After all, it's known as "The Peach State." Sweet Georgia peaches are juicy and unlike any other, which makes them just right for one of our favorite desserts - the peach cobbler. We especially love to make this during the summer, when Georgia's peaches are in season and are at their sweetest. Go ahead, be a peach and make this one for your family. They'll love you for it.

Serves 8

Ingredients

1 stick butter, melted

¾ cup water

2 cups sugar, divided

6 fresh peaches, peeled and sliced

¾ cup self-rising flour

¼ teaspoon salt

¾ cup milk

2 teaspoons ground cinnamon

Preparation

1 Preheat oven to 350 degrees F. Pour butter into a 9- x 13-inch baking dish; set aside.

2 In a medium saucepan over medium heat, combine water, 1 cup sugar, and the peaches; bring to a boil, then simmer 6 to 8 minutes or until peaches are tender. Using a slotted spoon, remove peaches to a bowl; reserve sugar mixture in saucepan.

3 Meanwhile, in a medium bowl, whisk flour, remaining 1 cup sugar, the salt, and milk until smooth. Slowly pour batter into baking dish. Arrange peach slices over batter (yes, over the batter), and stir cinnamon into reserved sugar mixture. Slowly pour the sugar mixture over the peach layer.

4 Bake 40 to 45 minutes or until mixture is bubbly and golden. Allow to cool slightly before serving warm.

Did You Know? No, we haven't gone bonkers in the Test Kitchen by putting the peaches on the top of the batter. You see, as this bakes, the peaches and the rich cinnamon syrup magically fall to the bottom, while the buttery layer rises to the top. If you'd like to make this even more magical, serve it with a scoop of ice cream.

Southerners' Favorite Banana Pudding

We're not about to start any arguments by saying that banana pudding belongs more to one state than another. Instead, we'll give credit to the entire Southern region for this one. It's Southerners who have made this creamy dessert an icon. From the banana pudding festivals of Tennessee to the church potlucks of Louisiana, this dessert has become a sweet staple at Southern tables.

Serves 8

Ingredients

CUSTARD

1-½ cups sugar, divided

¾ cup all-purpose flour

¼ teaspoon salt

6 eggs, separated

4 cups milk

2 teaspoons vanilla extract

1 (11-ounce) box vanilla wafer cookies

4 ripe bananas, sliced

Preparation

1 Preheat oven to 350 degrees F. To make Custard, combine 1 cup sugar, the flour, and salt in a large saucepan. Whisk in egg yolks and heat over medium heat until it forms a paste, stirring constantly. Reduce heat to low. Slowly whisk in milk until smooth. Cook 10 minutes or until thickened, whisking continuously. Remove from heat and stir in vanilla.

2 Spread a small amount of custard in a 2-quart casserole dish; cover with a layer of cookies, then top with a layer of banana slices. Spoon ⅓ of remaining custard over bananas and continue with layers, ending with custard.

3 To make meringue, in a large bowl with an electric mixer, beat the egg whites, gradually adding remaining ½ cup sugar, until soft peaks form. Spoon over top layer, spreading it evenly until the entire surface is covered and the edges are sealed.

4 Bake 10 to 15 minutes or until meringue is golden. Serve warm or refrigerate until ready to serve.

Bubblin' Blackberry Cobbler

Oregon is the top growing state for blackberries in the United States. In fact, some varieties of blackberries grow like weeds there; they're found practically everywhere. If you're a blackberry lover, then you've probably got a big smile on your face just thinking about the sticky fingers that you've gotten from eating them. For a less messy way to enjoy these fresh berries, try this warm and crusty cobbler. You'll never look back.

Serves 6

Ingredients

6 tablespoons butter, melted

¾ cup all-purpose flour

¾ cup plus 1 tablespoon sugar, divided

1-½ teaspoons baking powder

½ teaspoon salt

½ cup milk

1 teaspoon vanilla extract

1 teaspoon lemon juice

2 cups fresh blackberries

Preparation

1 Preheat oven to 350 degrees F. Pour butter into an 8-inch square baking dish.

2 In a medium bowl, whisk flour, ¾ cup sugar, the baking powder, and salt. Add milk, vanilla, and lemon juice, and whisk just until mixed. Pour batter slowly over butter. Place blackberries evenly on top of batter. Sprinkle with remaining 1 tablespoon sugar.

3 Bake 45 to 50 minutes or until golden.

Serving Suggestion: *Nothing goes better with this than a big scoop of vanilla ice cream. The tart warm berries are the perfect complement to the creamy vanilla ice cream.*

Date-Worthy Date Shakes

Who says you and your sweetie have to settle for the same old chocolate or vanilla milkshake every time? Why not shake things up with a date shake? After all, a date shake is the perfect shake to share with a date! In the U.S. dates are commonly grown in warm climates like Southern California, where they're loved and appreciated for being naturally sweet, just like you! Doesn't that make you want to blend one up right now?

Serves 2

Ingredients

½ cup pitted dates, coarsely chopped (4 to 5 dates)

½ cup cold milk, divided

2 large scoops vanilla ice cream

½ teaspoon vanilla extract

¼ teaspoon ground nutmeg

Whipped cream for garnish

Preparation

1 In a blender, combine dates and ¼ cup milk; blend on high until smooth. Add remaining ¼ cup milk, the ice cream, vanilla, and nutmeg. Blend on high until thoroughly mixed.

2 Divide evenly between 2 glasses. Garnish with whipped cream and serve immediately.

Did You Know? Dates are a good source of fiber, potassium, and iron. So, not only are they tasty, but they're also good for our overall wellbeing.

Colorado Bulldog

What do you get when you add some bubbles to a White Russian cocktail? A Colorado Bulldog! Supposedly named after one of the first unofficial mascots of Colorado State University, this spirited drink is perfect for someone with a sweet tooth. Some folks say it tastes like a milkshake. What do you think?

Serves 2

Ingredients

Ice cubes

3 ounces vodka

3 ounces coffee-flavored liqueur

2 ounces heavy cream

8 ounces cola soda

Preparation

1 Fill 2 tall glasses with ice cubes. Add vodka and liqueur to each glass, dividing evenly. Slowly pour half the heavy cream into each glass, then top each with cola. Stir and serve.

Recipes in Alphabetical Order

Recipes by Category

Recipes by Category

Recipes by Category

Recipes by Category